THE CHAMPION CODE

By Bruce & Diane Crevier

Presented to:

_____

The Champion Code
By Bruce and Diane Crevier

Copyright © 2015 by Bruce and Diane Crevier

All rights Reserved. No part of this publication may be reproduced, stored in a retrieval system, or transmitted by any means, electronic, mechanical, photographic (photocopying), recording, or otherwise, without prior permission in writing from the author.

ISBN: 978-0-692-37838-0

All Scripture verses cited are from the New King James Version.

Editors:
    Diane Crevier
    Bruce Crevier

Cover Design:
    Bruce Crevier

Page Layout, Interior Illustrations, Codes and Final Editing:
    Bruce Crevier
    Diane Crevier

To order additional copies:
championsforever.com

Coming in ebook format.

First Printing, February, 2015

Printed in the United States of America

"Have you ever met a family and said, *'I need to read the book they write?'* If not, you need to meet the Creviers. From the very first time we met Bruce and Diane and their amazing DOZEN, we knew the book you are holding HAD to be written. They will quickly tell you "It is Jesus in them", but I can tell you as their friend and former pastor, the CODES in this book are KEY to that happening in their lives and everyone who reads this great work. Our lives have been forever changed because of Jesus in them and we look forward to hearing how this book will awaken the Champion in you."   Pastor Tim and Kim Henderson, Entrepreneur, Former Pastor in Elkton, SD

"Jesus said, 'I have come that you might have life and that you might have it more abundantly.' What an incredible joy it has been to get to know the Crevier family who are great examples of the abundant life. My first introduction was through Tanya who soon introduced me to Bruce, Diane, and their precious children. They are truly champions and I am blessed every time I am with them. I have had the joy of watching every aspect of this book lived out in their entire family. Don't miss <u>The Champion Code</u>." Caz and Leslie McCaslin, Parents of three daughters, President/Founder Upward Unlimited

"I am thrilled to recommend Bruce Crevier's book, <u>The Champion Code</u>. I have had the privilege of knowing Bruce for years, and he and his family are the Real Deal! Reading this book will help you unlock the Champion Code and become a true Champion for Jesus Christ!" Pastor Eric Capaci, Husband, Father, Author, Pastor of Gospel Light Baptist Church, Founder of Champion Baptist College in Arkansas.

"The amazing Crevier family is unique in this world. Very rarely do you see such a large and talented family engaged in ministry together. Papa Bruce is a true man of God who shares his skills and message in a very simplistic yet powerful manner. Like the family that wrote it, this fun and entertaining book is uniquely simple, but very powerful! Everyone needs to read this book! It will captivate you; meet you where you are; and challenge you to go where you need to be!" Pastor Patrick Kimaiyo, Pastor of Redeemers House International, and Director of Messiah's Children - Kenya, Africa.

"Bruce is a Champion! He and his family have been commissioned by God to inspire, teach, equip and present the "Authentic Gospel" of Jesus Christ. Their ministry has impacted lives worldwide. I love

this book! These stories and examples both inspire and challenge. The Champion Code will absolutely touch you, provoke you, build your faith and cause you to both laugh and cry! This book will not only challenge you, but also cause you to believe for more of God in your own life." Scott and Janine (Crevier) Yoder, Parents of Six Children, Basketball Performer, and Inspirational Speaker.

"And they Overcame by the blood of the Lamb..." (Rev. 12:11) If you want to overcome, and if you believe in destiny for your life, then this book about God's hand in the life of Bruce and Diane Crevier and their family will change your life forever! Read and explore these stories, and you will see a pilgrimage of a life well spent!" Dr. Bert Brian Crevier, Author, Airline Transport Pilot, Gold Seal Flight Instructor, Inspirational Speaker.

"Bruce Crevier lives like a Champion and is one of the most positive people that I know. It is evident that he really loves and cares about people as he gives a lot of time and energy to help others out. This book is a reflection of what I am saying! Read this book with expectation as you discover that there is so much more for each of us to do and experience by living as Champions for Jesus!" Jim and Beth (Crevier) Harrison, Parents of seven children, Missionaries to Estonia and Bahrain.

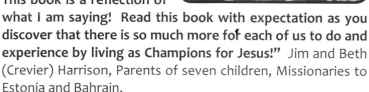

"God is pouring his Holy Spirit upon all mankind now! This book is a modern day book of Acts. Bruce and Diane have traveled extensively all over the world in the last 25 years using their talents to share the good news. They are living examples of being the hands and feet of the Savior! It has

been through their good times and bad times that God has divinely revealed to them the *Seven Things Champions Do Before They Die*. Every testimony is a miracle of walking out their faith in Jesus Christ!" Steve and Karen

(Crevier) Nelson, Parents of seven children, Entrepreneurs, Directors of Enoch Farm at **enochfarm.com**.

"The "Next Level", describes everything my brother, Bruce Crevier, is and does. God has blessed Bruce with amazing skills and talents. Bruce's book, The Champion Code is a "Next Level" unique way of challenging all of us to choose to live our lives like the True Champion - Jesus

Christ. You will be encouraged and inspired!" Tanya Crevier, World's Best Female Basketball Handler, Performer and Inspirational Speaker, Member of The South Dakota Sports Hall of Fame and FCA Hall of Fame -

tanyacrevier.com

First Timothy 4:15-16 says: "Meditate on these things; give yourself entirely to them, that your progress may be evident to all. Take heed to yourself and to the doctrine. Continue in them, for in doing this, you will save both yourself and those who hear you." Heed the words of this man of God

and you will be blessed as I have. Ray Crevier, United States Naval Academy Graduate, Navy Jet Pilot for 20 years, Currently an International Pilot for Delta Airlines.

It was said of two Kings of Judah "...and as long as he sought the Lord, God made him prosper." And "...he became mighty because he directed his ways in the ways of the Lord his God." Like these examples, Bruce and Diane, are a mighty man and woman of God who prosper and represent the Lord's greatness. Consequently, this book is worth standing up and taking notice! I highly recommend this book. It is a message for those who are searching, and for all who love God. Teresa Crevier, Worship Leader, Pianist, Recording Artist, Author

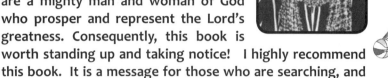

"You are created to be a Champion! Bruce Crevier shares seven undeniable qualities that will help you achieve new levels of success. Get these deep down inside, and boldly go in the direction of your calling!" Marc and Sandy Crevier - Parents of five children, National Motor Club Number One Salesman, Member of Ashland University Football Hall of Fame.

People will be blessed by this book! The reason? Because this book has been built on the solid foundation that was started by our parents, Raymond and Patricia Crevier, who raised their family to seek and to follow the Lord. Maurice and Rita Crevier - Parents of four children, Entrepreneur, Carpenter, Health Coach, Member of Ashland University Football Hall of Fame.

THANK YOU

If you see a turtle on the top of a fencepost, what can you know? One thing is for certain, he must have had a lot of help in getting there because turtles can't climb! In the same way, any success that we have had, we had a lot of help along the way. We want to give credit to where credit is due. There are many people who have been instrumental in shaping our lives and helping with this ministry and this project. We want to take time to thank them:

The Crevier Family, with Bruce in front next to his sister Janine.

To my parents, Patricia and Raymond Crevier (both deceased), and Diane's parents, Carol and Neil Athow, who unselfishly raised twelve and seven children, respectively. Thank you for raising us and instilling within us a desire to love and follow God; the art of self-sacrifice; and for encouraging us in the midst of our faults.

To Diane's six brothers and sisters: Mike, Fran, Julie, Janet, Mark and Amy. To my eleven brothers and sisters: Marty (deceased), Maurice, Marc, Teresa, Ray, Tanya, Karen, Beth, Bert, Ann, and Janine. Thank you for being our best friends and for being great examples.

We want to thank our Board of Directors, Ron Borchardt, and Jon Henrich for your wisdom. We are also indebted to our many brothers and sisters in Christ across the country. (You know who you are.) Thank you for your prayers and support. Because of you, we are able to bring the good news to so many!

Diane, front left, with her mom, dad, brothers and sisters.

Last, but certainly not least, we dedicate this book to God the Father, Jesus Christ His Son, and the Holy Spirit. Thank You for the gift of life, and for giving Your life for us! Thank You that Your tomb is empty and that You are alive forevermore! Thank You for adopting us and showing us how to truly love.

In Israel with Katie and Isaiah, in the empty Tomb!

THE NARROW BRIDGE
By Bruce Crevier

A couple was surely traveling, on a lonely narrow road,
They came to a giant chasm, and put down their heavy load.
The chasm was so wide, and also very deep,
The narrow road went down the cliff, and was also very steep.
Too dangerous for travel, and not for the weary soul.
They contemplated the danger, and then decided to go.
So they ventured down the cliff, to the valley of the shadow,
And almost fell from fear, into the deepest dark meadow.
They climbed the other side, and barely made it still
And paused for a weary moment, to see just how they feel.
Then looking back below, at the fearful, ugly trail,
They thought of those behind; would they fail or prevail?
They decided then to stay, and build a narrow bridge.
Over the giant chasm, just on top of the lonely ridge.
The couple kept on working, and labored day and night,
People would pass by, wondering if this was right.
While the couple was still building, the questions would arise.
What's with all the labor, is this so no one dies?
Yes, it seems so very crazy, to build a silly bridge,
On top of this giant chasm, and across this lonely ridge,
But the reason that we labor so hard in this place
Is because we have a family, and only by God's grace.
Our family will be traveling, along this narrow road,
And when they get this far, they will have a heavy load.
To travel through this Chasm, will be difficult indeed
We do not want to lose one, but help them in their need.
So we have been here building, and working very hard,
Just to see them make it, without too many scars.
The prize that will come, to all our kids you see,
Is to see them cross this bridge, to see them full and free.
When our kids cross this bridge, our hearts will see their joy,
Knowing that our labor, was for our girls and boys.
This bridge will also be, a help for others who come,
For those who travel this narrow road, are looking for freedom.
The reason that we wrote, the book that you now hold,
Is for our kids and others, for the young and old.
God has shown us things that will help those in need.
To help them with their journey, to help them to succeed.
We wrote them down on paper, for all the world to see,
That God will make them Champions, and give them victory.
So you will cross that Chasm, 'cuz we have gone before,
To build the bridge you see, to show God's grace and more.

TABLE OF CONTENTS

Recommendations.. 3
Thank you... 8
Poem "The Narrow Bridge.. 10
Foreword... 12
Introduction... 14

Code #1 - Champions make sure their name is in the Book of Life
Story... 21
Application... 30

Code #2 - Champions get to know Jesus Christ the One Who Died for Them!
Story... 51
Application... 62

Code #3 - Champions make Jesus Christ Known to the World
Story #1 71
Story #2.. 80
Application... 93

Code #4 - Champions Build Their Lives on the Rock of God's Word
Story... 107
Application... 118

Code #5 - Champions Become Overcomers by Defeating Temptations and Trials
Story... 125
Application... 165

Code #6 - Champions Show Love by Giving to God and Others
Story... 175
Application... 192

Code #7 - Champions Take Care of the Gifts that God has given them.
Story... 199
Application... 205

Champions Choose the Difficult Path
Confessions of Champions..................................... 209

Side Bar Animations...1 - 224

FOREWORD
THE CHAMPION CODE

The Champion Code is written by a man who lives life as a champion for Christ. Bruce Crevier is the single most influential person for Christ I have had the privilege to know. The power and motivation behind that influence comes from his daily walk with Jesus. It is easy to talk about living for Christ, but it is something else entirely another to actually do it.

When I met Bruce in college, I was lost. I thought I knew God, but I did not know Him in a personal way. My sins had not yet been forgiven. I remember one dark night in my dorm room when I was struggling with the meaning of life. It felt like I was the only person in the universe as I sat under my lofted bed thinking about why I was always so unhappy. I felt empty inside. Just then, I noticed a Bible on a shelf next to the chair where I was sitting. Instinctively, I knew it had the answers. I picked it up and began to read.

After a few minutes my heart began to get angry. Not one word on those pages made any sense to me. I sat looking at that Bible and felt the rage build. Suddenly I exploded. I threw the Bible across the dorm room. It hit the door and fell to the floor splitting into pieces. Defeated, I fell to my knees and cried out, "God! I just want to know You!"

About a month later, I was sitting in that same dorm room when my Resident Assistant walked in. Ron came to tell me about an RA job that had just opened. I did not want the job, but I quickly became interested when he told me it paid room and board. Later that day I found myself moving my things up to the third floor of the dorm to be the new RA.

I walked towards my new room, number 330. Along the way I passed room number 329. On the door was a sign with a Bible verse that said, **"I am the way, the truth and the life, the only way to the Father is through Me" (John 14:6).**

I had no idea that God was about to answer the prayer I had cried out to Him that dark night in my dorm room a month earlier.

Curious about the Bible verse, I knocked on the door to meet my new neighbor. Bruce Crevier opened the door. I introduced myself as his new RA, and I was surprised by the first thing he said to me as he reached out to shake my hand. "Hey, are you a Christian?" he asked.

That sums up the author of The Champion Code. In the past thirty years of knowing Bruce, it seems his first thought on any subject is Jesus. He lives and breathes his relationship with Jesus Christ. Everything he does has Jesus right in the middle of it. While I have known Bruce, I have been fortunate to travel with him all over the world on ministry trips. I have personally seen him preach the love of Jesus and lead countless people, young and old, to a saving knowledge of Jesus Christ.

That laser focus on Jesus is what brought about The Champion Code. It is not just a book written for entertainment. Although very entertaining, every word was written with the purpose, prayer, and hope that it will guide fellow believers in their relationship and walk with God.

Although distractions constantly chip away at our commitments to the important things in life, The Champion Code will help make Jesus your number one priority. Luke 9:23 says, "If anyone wishes to follow after Me, he must deny himself, and take up his cross daily and follow Me."

For anyone who is serious about following Jesus, The Champion Code is one of the greatest tools ever found. Each of the seven codes is uniquely established straight out of God's Word to build a strong foundation for God's work in your life. With a doubt, The Champion Code will inspire you to run like a champion for Christ! **Bret and Marie Merkle, Parents of Five Children, Author of Tragic Blessing, Inspirational Speaker, Attorney, go to tragicblessing.com**

Bret & Marie Merkle

INTRODUCTION

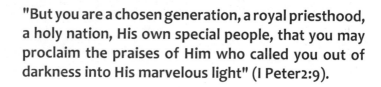

"But you are a chosen generation, a royal priesthood, a holy nation, His own special people, that you may proclaim the praises of Him who called you out of darkness into His marvelous light" (I Peter 2:9).

My wife and I were walking through a store a few years ago, and we saw a book entitled, <u>100 Movies You Must See Before You Die</u>. After we read the title of that book, we came to the conclusion that although movies can be fun to watch, there was a greater cause that needed attention besides just watching movies. That "Greater Cause" is the reason for this book!

In your hand is a book filled with true stories about what it means to be a Champion, called **The Champion Code**. If you never see those 100 movies; don't worry, you won't miss a thing. But if you do not do the **Seven Things That Champions Do Before They Die**, then you will miss out on being truly loved and blessed in this life, and you may miss heaven and its blessings in the life to come!

But really, who are we to write a book about Champions? I am going to tell who we are. We are nobodies who don't know anything, telling you about SOMEONE who knows everything! They call him the King of Kings. His name is Jesus.

Now I know what some of you are thinking. This is going to be another boring book about religion, right? Sorry to disappoint you, for this is not just another book about some boring religion. Rather, an exciting adventure book about a relationship with the living God, who is the King of Glory!

You see my friends, something so fantastic has happened in our lives that God has given us a message for you! This message starts and ends with what it means to know a Divine Being who just happens to be Someone similar to you and me, for the Scripture says we are made in the image of God, and this God knows you very well.

Now concerning God, as you read this book, you will be in one of three boats. You either love Him, or you hate Him, or you just plain don't care! Whatever boat you are in it doesn't matter. For whether you believe it or not, the fact remains: God the Father sent His Son Jesus to this earth! This Jesus actually lived, died and rose again; and in the process, He split time and changed all of history. Yes, it is HIS-Story. How do I know? Today's date is taken from Him, and He changed my life and my entire family!

But the good news doesn't stop there. This awesome God loves you so much that at this moment He is allowing you to read a book dedicated to Him!

You see, this book is not about me or my family, it is about Him. We are characters in the drama of these true stories, but as you will soon see, God's unseen hand is the one pulling the strings. He made these unbelievable events happen like they did. You will not be receiving secondhand information of God's workings. **These will be firsthand accounts of God's divine hand on an ordinary family striving to serve an extraordinary GOD!**

So what is a Champion? Here's the definition of a Champion:

> **cham·pi·on 1. One that wins first place or first prize in a competition. 2. One that is clearly superior or has the attributes of a winner. 3. An ardent defender or supporter of a cause or another person: a champion of the homeless. 4. One who fights; a warrior.**
> The American Heritage® Dictionary of the English Language, Fourth Edition copyright ©2000 by Houghton Mifflin Company.

We have all heard of state champions, national champions, Olympic champions, and the list goes on and on. Everyone loves to watch champions, and we all love it best when we *are* the Champion. God has put that Champion desire in our hearts. **You see, God wins at everything He does. He invented prosperity, success, and is the epitome of a Champion. He is not just a Champion, He is THE CHAMPION!** Do you not think that the inventor of the word Champion will not want the same for His children. Of course He does! He wants you follow in His footsteps and be like Him.

But you see, many of you are not lucky enough to be a Champion, because becoming a Champion only happens to "lucky" people, right? I get that all the time. "Oh, you are so lucky to travel around and perform with your family." I want you to know, there is no such thing as luck. Luck is defined as **"success or failure apparently brought on by chance, rather than one's own actions."** What has happened to us is not by chance, for there has been and continues to be a Divine Hand working in our lives, as you will see.

If you notice, most little kids think they are champions. It is in their nature! Everyone starts with a desire to succeed, and most have big dreams to do something positive with their lives. We have met older people who use to have those same dreams, but today they are in their 40s, 50s, 60s, and beyond, and they are still trying to figure out what they want to become when they grow up. The problem is this, they met with resistance and didn't reach their dreams.

Maybe as you read these words, you can relate. As a child, maybe you really honestly tried to succeed, but circumstances were against you. When you looked in the mirror, you felt like you are too short or too tall, too skinny or too fat, wrong color hair or skin, too little hair, too much hair. Maybe you had people discourage you; maybe you felt bullied or felt you weren't as talented as you thought. Maybe you are dealing with a tragedy that left you crippled or maimed. Maybe you were abused as a child and never truly knew the unconditional love of a father and a mother. Maybe some you are reading these words as you sit in a jail cell, trying to figure out life and trying to figure out what went wrong. You want to get out of the prison of your heart! If you can relate with any of these examples, I praise God for you right where you are, for there is HOPE!!

The bad news is you can't change where you are coming from, but the good news is you can certainly change where you are going! You can't do much about your ancestors, but you can influence your descendants enormously. Every person who reads this book can become what eludes most people, for this is a book of hope for those who would like to be on the **REAL** Championship Team and, most importantly, be **TRUE** champions themselves.

I prayed to God, "God, show me what we need to do before we die!" So armed with a prayer and my Bible, I set out to decipher **The Champion Code**. The Lord revealed to me seven things that we all need to do before we die. **After you die, you won't have another chance! These seven codes are for this earth and have been decoded for you.** If you have never read the Bible before, or even if you are a Bible scholar, this will cut through the red tape and answer the question: What do I need to do right now to make my life count on earth and for eternity?

My daughter, Hollie, loves to knit and also loves to do cross-stitch with a needle and thread. She made a beautiful cross-stitch design with flowers and wrote a Bible verse on the bottom. When I looked at her cross-stitch design from the top, it was beautiful. But when I flipped the cross-stitch over and looked at the bottom, all I saw was an ugly mess of twisted thread that didn't look at all like the top. The top was orderly and beautiful, but the bottom was the total opposite. It was this chaos of twisted thread that made the top look so good.

In the same way, when we look at our life from

man's perspective, things can look really ugly. That's the bad news. But when we look at things from God's angle, we see what God sees; it is a beautiful work of art! In this book, you are going to see a lot of twisted thread, but God has made (and continues to make) a beautiful design as we look at it from His perspective.

Welcome to **The Champion Code.** It is our prayer that these words will inspire, encourage, and challenge you to be the Champion that God wants you to be! So if you are up for the challenge, then open your heart and get ready to let God work in your life. These pages will show you how to: 1) start thinking like a Champion, 2) start talking like a Champion, 3) start acting like a Champion.

My family and I have been praying for every Champion who reads this book, so I guess that looks like you! Enjoy this book and remember: GO FOR IT!

We Love YOU!

Bruce and Diane Crevier

THE BROOKINGS REGISTER

ASTORIA AURORA BROOKINGS BRUCE BUSHNELL COLMAN EGAN ELKTON ESTELLINE FLANDREAU NUNDA RUTLAND SINAI

One family's balancing act

■ The entire Crevier family of Elkton gets in on unique basketball-unicycle show

By Charis Prunty
The Brookings Register

BROOKINGS – When their oldest son Jacob was old enough to walk, Elkton resident Bruce Crevier would pull him out of the crowd at a show and have him hold up a finger, then balance a spinning basketball on it.

"We never dreamed that we'd have 12 kids and we would be traveling all over the place as a family," Bruce said. "I mean, I started out just doing it all by myself and, as the kids grew up, they of course learned and I incorporated them into the program."

Twenty-one years ago, Bruce and Diane Crevier made Bruce's passion for entertaining and teaching into their full-time work, and named it Champions Forever Ministries. The ministry is a nonprofit organization that takes this family to schools, community events, half-time shows, prisons and just about anywhere. Recently the Creviers have won national recognition as contenders on the television show America's Got Talent.

Bruce comes from a family of 12 kids himself; he's the 11th. His siblings were active in sports and, when his brothers learned in college how to spin a basketball on their finger, they came home and taught their sister Tanya. She's since become a star basketball handler.

Bruce is 10 years younger than Tanya and, when he was 6 or 7, he decided he wanted to learn that skill, too. Then in sixth grade he learned to ride a unicycle, when his cousin Lance brought over a unicycle for the day and, seeing Bruce's enthusiasm to ride it, gave it to him.

Basketball skills and unicycling became the core of Bruce's show, which he began doing during college. After college he was working full-time and doing shows on the side, but they gathered momentum and a point came when he and Diane had to choose whether to go full-time with it.

See **CREVIERS**, page A2

Courtesy photo

While Elkton residents Bruce and Diane Crevier and family have come into the spotlight this month as contestants on America's Got Talent, the family has been practicing and performing full-time as Champions Forever Ministries for 21 years. This family includes: Top row, Bruce and Diane; second row from left: Isaiah, Jacob and Caleb; third row: Katie, Josiah and Hollie; fourth row: Zach, Ben and Micah; bottom row: Tessa, Nathan and Tori.

Officials probe jet f... too ...

By Jason Dearen
Associated Press

SAN FRANC... have determined 214 was traveling get speed during crew tried to abo... smashed onto the the type of aircraft port played a role...

A day after the Francisco, killing more than 180 ... Sunday that the p... whether the airpor... could have malfun...

The South Kor... Monday that offici... landing equipmen...

SDSU co-ch... nat'l comm...

BROOKINGS – Dakota State Un... research, was rece... federal biomass r... served on since M...

Members o... Biomass Resea... Development I... Technical A... Committee expertise in the biomass energy an... the U.S. Departm... Agriculture Department of En... fulfilling their obli... for a section of the Bill called the B...

Driver in Elkt... area r...

ELKTON – Alco... gle-vehicle rollover Elkton early Sunda... the Brookings Coun...

The driver of the injured after his pic... way, hit the ditch an... side fence.

The accident too... Sunday on Highway ...

The deputy's re... Fernando Corado-r...

19

Courtesy photo

Champions Forever, made up of the Elkton-based Crevier family, performs during half-time of a basketball game.

CREVIERS: Family travels half year

Continued from page A1

(Diane fit right in: When she met Bruce, she already could spin a basketball. While she has stayed busy caring for their family and home-schooling the kids, Diane took time 13 years ago to learn to ride a unicycle herself.)

When they started Champions Forever 21 years ago, they had three little boys. Now they have 12 kids: Jacob, 25 (who is married to Alicia and has two children of his own); Caleb, 24; Isaiah, 22; Katie, 20; Josiah, 17; Hollie, 15; Ben, 13; Micah, 11; Zach, 9; Nathan, 6; and Tori and Tessa, 4-year-old twins.

All of them can ride a unicycle, ranging in height from just a couple feet off the ground to 10 feet tall. And while they can all put a finger in the air to hold a spinning basketball, it still takes some serious practice to learn to spin the ball for themselves, and to do other tricks.

Training

When the kids have turned 4 years old, Bruce has spent about 30 minutes per day teaching them to ride a unicycle. Tori and Tessa rode their unicycles in their first show earlier last month. During an interview Friday, they rode around the family's living room.

"This is a normal occurrence in our house – we'll be cooking supper and they'll be riding around us," Katie said.

"You'll back into them – you know, you'll turn around and they'll be there," Diane said.

Bruce builds the 10-foot giraffe unicycles himself. There's too much liability in them for a company to sell them, he said, because they're so high off the ground.

"But we've never gotten hurt on a unicycle or anything. A scraped-up knee is about as bad as it gets," Hollie said.

"They look dangerous but, surprisingly, no one's ever gotten hurt," Bruce added. "But by the time they're on these (a 10-footer), they've gotten so good at those (short unicycles) that they know how to land if something goes wrong."

The best way to land is on your feet, Katie said. Once the rider hits that "point of no return" where they know they can't correct their movements, they let themselves fall. It's eight feet from their feet to the ground on the tallest cycles.

Katie and her three older brothers are out of high school now: Jacob has his own jewelry business, Caleb and Isaiah recently graduated from South Dakota State University and Katie currently attends there. They now choose when to travel with the family, and when to practice. Practice time depends on the week and how busy it is, Katie said.

"You just kind of come down the stairs and it's like, 'Oh, I'll practice a little bit today.' I mean, it's not really a set time," Katie said.

Performing with the family is really a job for the kids, too, they said. Some of the older kids take other jobs, but they tell their employers up front that they sometimes travel with their family, and their employers have been very flexible about scheduling.

Flexibility also comes from having several pre-planned shows: Bruce by himself, Bruce with two or three others, the whole family together and sometimes the family minus Bruce. They also join with their aunt Tanya Crevier sometimes: She lives in Elkton and has her own ministry based on basketball-handling skills, called Enthusiasm International.

Altogether, the family spends about 150 days per year on the road, though Bruce is on the road about 200-220 days per year himself. The family travels mainly in its commercial-sized tour bus, inside which they built bunk beds for everyone to sleep while traveling.

The point

Asked what the goal of Champion Forever is, and you'll understand how much thought this family has put into its ministry. Rather than simply entertaining, they use the platform to encourage people to "become champions in the game of life." Bruce quotes motivational author and speaker Zig Ziglar, who said, "Success is when opportunity meets preparation."

"I ask kids all the time, 'What are you doing right now to prepare yourself for the opportunities that God is going to be giving you?' And to give you an example, this 'America's Got Talent' that we're doing, this is an opportunity that's been presented to us, but I feel like I've been preparing my whole life to do stuff just like this," he said.

The Creviers also want to teach priorities: God first, others second and yourself last.

"Because I find in my life if I get my priorities out of order, that if I get my priorities back in order it makes my life a lot more meaningful," Bruce said.

In public schools, where they aren't free to speak openly about God, they focus on encouraging students to make good choices.

"We encourage kids to set goals, have the right attitude – you know, if bad things happen to you, it might not actually be all that bad. Because a lot of opportunities are disguised as obstacles in your life," Bruce said.

They also encourage others to have a high standard for themselves and live a moral life. Bruce, Diane and the older kids have all performed their show in prisons, where they've met people who look highly educated and successful but have made wrong choices. They encourage these prisoners to begin making the right choices, and encourage students to make good choices so they don't end up there.

The family has its own goal, too: To know God and make him known. They see their opportunity to make a living by playing basketball and riding unicycles as a blessing from God.

"It's not because I'm anything special, but because I serve a special God," Bruce said. "He's in the business of doing extraordinary things through ordinary people. We're just an ordinary family – we happen to have 12 kids; that might not be ordinary," he said, pausing as everyone laughed.

"But everything that we do has been a miracle. I just give all the credit to God – he's No. 1. He gives us true joy in life."

Learn more about the Creviers and see their performance schedule at championsforever.com or www.facebook.com/foreverchampions. Watch them perform on "America's Got Talent" during the Vegas round, July 16 and 17 on NBC.

Contact Charis Prunty at cprunty-@brookingsregister.com.

Code #1

CODE #1
CHAMPIONS MAKE SURE THEIR NAME IS IN THE BOOK OF LIFE

"And anyone not found written in the Book of Life was cast into the lake of fire" (Rev. 20:15).

"I would rather live my life as if there is a God, then die, and find out that there isn't. Than to live my life as if there isn't a God, only to die to find out that there is!"
Author Unknown

STORY:
DEATH, POUNDING AT THE DOOR

"DIANE, WE HAVE NO BRAKES! WE HAVE NO BRAKES! I CAN'T SLOW DOWN!" I screamed to my wife as we were headed down a Colorado mountain pass on I-80. We were in our motorhome with the whole family and we couldn't stop! As I stomped on the brakes, there was no response from the brake pedal and we were headed for stopped cars in the middle of the interstate! We were surrounded by steep mountains and we were picking up speed.

The smell of burning brakes filled our motorhome. I wished it were only a dream, but this frightening nightmare was actually happening. My family and I were confronted with the reality that in less than thirty seconds something horrible was about to take place. DEATH WAS POUNDING AT THE DOOR! When you are face to face with death with no time to pray, what do you do?

The true story I just described takes place in the early fall of 2003. To give you a little background, we were headed west on Interstate 80 (I-80). I was driving our loaded-down, 36-foot Class A motorhome, pulling a 16-foot enclosed trailer across the country from our home in South Dakota. In all, our motorhome and our trailer weighed over 14 tons.

It was a hot fall day, and we were headed to California. We were scheduled to do programs for a local church, and also some school assembly programs in the Modesto, California, area. My family and I were looking forward to our time, for we were going to see some friends that we had met the year before. Our little ones at the time--Josiah, Hollie, Ben, and Micah--were taking naps in the back. Caleb and Isaiah were playing a game on the dinette table; Katie was sitting on the couch reading a book; and Jacob, our oldest, was sitting up front with my wife, Diane, looking out the window.

"Hey, Diane, look at these mountains?" I said as we were driving through the majestic mountains of Colorado.

"I can see why people would like to live here," Diane said as we all gazed at the majestic scenery.

While driving to the top of the mountain, the scenery was breathtaking. As we came over the top and headed back down, I noticed a caution sign that read:

STEEP DOWNGRADE - 7% GRADE
NEXT 4 MILES - TRUCKS USE LOWER GEAR

Having driven through the mountains many times before, I gladly heeded the caution and shifted our motorhome down to second gear.

Things were going fine, and then about a half mile down the pass, we noticed stopped cars and trucks with another sign. This was a road construction sign that read:

ROAD CONSTRUCTION
NEXT 4 MILES
ONE LANE ROAD AHEAD

All the cars ahead of us were either stopped or going really slow because there was a bottleneck up ahead on the road. It turned out to be a large traffic jam in the middle of this steep downgrade on Interstate 80. Both lanes were completely full of cars. We would stop for a while and then slowly drive forward for about 100 yards, only to stop again to accommodate all the cars.

"Hey, Diane, you don't see this too often. It looks like we have a traffic jam in the middle of the mountains," I said.

"We'll just have to enjoy looking at these big mountains," Isaiah, our third son, added as we stopped.

"The view is something else and reminds me of growing up in Spearfish," Diane said, thinking about her upbringing in the Black Hills of South Dakota.

"Yes, it sure would be a beautiful place to live!" I responded.

Because God had done so much for us, we had a desire to do something for Him. When we first got married, Diane and I asked God to make a way so that we could travel and share His message to the world. He was answering that prayer by giving us opportunities to perform and share the love of Christ both individually and also as a family.

It was fun getting to travel as a family, but anybody with a family knows traveling with the whole family was a lot of extra work. Even though it was difficult, it was proving to be a blessing. With our growing family becoming more a part of the "Spin-tacular Basketball Show" we were finding that it was affecting our audiences in ways that we never would have imagined. We were getting letters from people of all walks of life saying that they were very encouraged by seeing a family work together. We were so thankful for God's leading and provision! Plus, all this traveling together was making us a close-knit family.

Back to the mountains, it was about 20 minutes later, and we were still stopping and starting, moving slowly down the mountain pass. The stopping and starting over and over was getting me a little concerned since we still had three miles left of this 7% downgrade, and it was a hot day in Colorado.

"Hey, Diane, wow! Look at those two truckers up ahead on the shoulder of the road. Their brakes are so hot that smoke is billowing out from behind the wheels," I said as we passed by them.

For the next few moments, I pondered their grim situation. This stop-and-go traffic jam was heating up everyone's brakes, and those truckers were the sad victims of this "out of the ordinary" traffic situation.

"That's too bad. I wonder if my brakes are getting hot," I said to Diane as I was once again pressing on my brakes.

"Bruce, can you smell that?" Diane asked with a concerned look on her face.

I knew immediately what it was. It was the smell of hot brakes. In my mind, I wanted that smell to be coming from the truckers that we passed, but the more we drove, the more I realized that the smell was not the truckers. It was our brakes.

"That smell is coming from our brakes, Diane. I better try and let them cool off," I said.

So when we came up to the traffic, I stopped with my main foot brake and engaged our parking brake by pulling out a yellow switch on the dash. This is a totally separate brake located on the drive shaft of the motorhome. When I engaged it, I was able to release my foot brake to let the main brakes cool off. When traffic got about 200 - 300 yards ahead of us, I disengaged the parking brake and gravity would make us coast up to the traffic where I again applied my main brakes to stop. I then reapplied the parking brake to hold the motorhome while I tried to let the main brakes cool off. We did this technique a couple times, and I thought it was helping the main brakes cool off, but I was totally mistaken!

On our third time, I let up the parking brake as before, and we started coasting toward the stopped cars ahead. I went to apply pressure on the main brakes and, to my horror my foot went all the way to the floor and the motor home didn't stop! It all happened so fast! As I glanced down at my gauges, I was startled by a brand new red light flashing in front of me that said "BRAKES(!)" with a new warning sound. It was going, "BEEEEEEEEP"! I had never seen this light or heard that sound before. Could my brakes be GONE? I thought.

Again and again I pushed down on the main brake

pedal, and the pedal went all the way to the floor. I quickly started pumping the brakes with no response, and my heart sank! I thought to myself is this really happening? I kept pushing and still no response! I started frantically stomping on the brake pedal and still nothing!

"Diane, my brakes are not working!" I shouted!

"What? Bruce! What?" Diane said in a puzzled manner from the passenger seat.

"My brakes are not responding! WHEN I PUSH DOWN, THERE IS NO RESPONSE! THEY ARE GONE!" I yelled while I continued stomping.

I was frantically pumping and stomping the brakes and still there was no response. In desperation I engaged the parking brake. Still no response! I looked out my rear view mirrors and to my horror, the same white smoke that I had seen from the truckers wheels was now billowing out both sides of the motorhome's back fender wheel wells! We were moving quickly toward the stopped cars ahead and we were picking up speed! If we could smell burning brakes before, we could really smell it now for the smell was filling the motorhome! Fear gripped our hearts and we were confronted with what Psalms 23 portrays "the valley of the shadow of death"! Ours was a valley headed for disaster!

In an effort to slow down the motorhome with only seconds to spare, I started steering the big rig left and right, zig-zagging as much as I could without smashing any cars to the left of me and before I reached the stopped cars in front of me. Still, NOTHING WAS WORKING AND WE WERE SLOWLY PICKING UP SPEED!

As I looked ahead, we had at least fifty stopped cars less than 100-yards in front of us. We were rapidly closing in on them and crossing a bridge at the same time. As I quickly scanned the area, we had mountains with trees that were surrounding us. The mountain on the right side of the road shot up 1000-feet. To the left of the road, it went down a 500-foot ravine. Up ahead were stopped cars and construction workers. There was no way out!

"DIANE, I CAN'T SLOW DOWN!" I yelled.

When there is no time to pray, what do you do? We cried the only name that can do anything in a hopeless situation! Both Diane and I began to yell, "JESUS! HELP US! JESUS! HELP US!

On the bridge I was zig-zagging the motorhome in order to try to gain more time and to help slow it down. I had never felt so utterly helpless in a hopeless situation! As I looked ahead, thoughts were flying through my mind. There did not seem to be a happy ending to this situation. If I were sleeping and this was a nightmare, now would be a good time to wake up! But this living NIGHTMARE was not going away! If I went right I would hit the trees and the mountain, if I went left I would smash cars and go down a 500-foot ravine. If I went forward I would plow into those cars. The realization came to me that people were going to get hurt and potentially DIE. Some of those people were going to be my FAMILY and ME! Crying out to Jesus was the only thing that we could do, so Diane and I continued our cry to the Lord. "JESUS PLEASE HELP US! JESUS PLEASE HELP US!"

It was at that moment that the Lord directed my eyes to the right side of the road. As I crossed the bridge, I noticed amongst the mountains and trees, but blocked from my view until after the bridge, there was a small clearing in the trees. The area looked somewhat clear to the right. It had a four-foot ditch but went up from there to an embankment before it shot straight up the mountain. Everything was happening so fast that I hardly had time to think! I didn't want to smash into the cars ahead of me, and I certainly didn't want to drive over the edge of the mountain and lose my family. So when I saw the steep embankment, I was seconds from smashing into the cars in front of us, so I just looked at Diane and shouted with a firm emphasis, "SHOULD I TAKE IT?"

Diane looked to the right where I was looking and with great desperation shouted, "TAKE IT!"

That was all the confirmation I needed, so I ceased from zig-zagging, quickly turned the steering wheel and drove our motorhome and trailer off the road narrowly missing the stopped cars in front of us!

As we drove off the road, we angled down the ditch, veering up the mountain embankment, and then we headed up the steep mountain! It was so frightening as we could feel the top of the motorhome beginning to lean to the left. It was leaning more, and more, and then even more! Because of the steep angle of the embankment, I was ready for the whole thing to tip over!

We came to an abrupt stop, and I shouted to the kids, "Everyone get to the right side of the motorhome, NOW!" I did this to shift as much of the weight as possible to the right to stabilize the motorhome. To this day, I still cannot believe we didn't tip over. It was almost as if the hand of God was keeping us from tipping.

With my family plastered on the right wall inside of the motorhome, we all gasped because even though we were stopped, we were leaning so much everyone was still anticipating something to happen. Everything was quiet for 30 seconds and then everyone forced a sigh of relief. We quickly said a prayer of thanks to God for getting us past the first obstacle.

Now that we were off the road and up the mountain, we were confronting another mountain of impossibility. What do we do next?

I slowly got out and checked the motorhome. To my utter amazement other than some cracked fiberglass on the bottom of the front right corner, there was virtually no damage at all. We were about fifty-yards off Interstate 80 with our motorhome angled up the mountain in an area that seemed to be awkwardly perfect for what took place. Every place within 100-yards of this area could have destroyed the motorhome and could have hurt and killed some people. God's provision caused us to pause and thank Him for this natural landscape formation that stopped us! We thanked and thanked God for getting us stopped!

We were able to find out our location and called a tow truck. About an hour later, a large truck used for towing semi trucks came to our rescue. He hooked his long cable winch onto our trailer and slowly pulled us backwards off the mountain embankment to the shoulder of I-80. Because of the angle, the mountain, and the ditch, it took a total of 4 hours to do this and cost us $650 for the tow truck, but we were so thankful to God to be back on the road.

By 11:00 pm the tow truck driver had gotten us off the mountain and all the traffic was gone. While on the side of the road, we checked and rechecked the brakes and they were responding as if nothing happened. With no traffic, we carefully followed the tow truck driver down the mountain and then headed on our way. To our surprise, we had no further incidence with our brakes!

An hour later, we stopped at a truck stop down the road and everything that happened was still racing through my mind. For the rest of that trip, I had weird feelings and thoughts of what could have happened but didn't! I really felt like that was the end for us and that we were going to be standing before God that day. For a while, it was difficult to sleep at night, but God gave me peace. We were so thankful that we had a God in heaven who watches out for His children.

APPLICATION: WHERE IS YOUR NAME WRITTEN?

My family and I will never forget that close brush with death! I hope you never have to go through a hopeless and fearful situation like that. But there is one unpleasant situation that each of us will have to contend with someday. There is a 100% chance that everyone will DIE. From what we know, all of us are going to be dead for a very long time! There are two questions that need an answer: "When will it happen?" and "Where is our name written?"

GUINNESS BOOK OF WORLD RECORDS

Have you ever had a great day? Think of one of the best days in your life. I had a day like that.

The second time I broke the world record for basketball spinning, they put my picture in The Guinness Book of World Records, on page 223, and on the SAME PAGE with Michael Jordan, one of the greatest basketball players of all time! (See Picture) For me, that was a GREAT DAY! They even put my picture on the top of the page, and Michael Jordan's picture was on the bottom of the page!

A few weeks after that great day, I was laying in bed thinking about how cool it was to have my name and picture in The Guinness Book of Records, and I felt pride build up in my heart. Then out of the blue, I felt God speaking to my heart. He said, "Bruce, don't be glad your name is written The Guinness Book of Records, because that book means nothing to Me. Be glad that your name is written in the Book of Life."

"Was that God?" I thought as I pondered those words. So I grabbed my Bible, and I looked up the verse that talks about the Book of Life. It says: **"Anyone whose name was not found written in the book of life was cast into the lake of fire"** (Rev. 20:15).

After I read that, it hit me! Having my name in The Guinness Book of Records means nothing! The Book of Life is the most important book to have my name in. When I put this accomplishment into perspective, I realized that God allowed me to get into a famous earthly book, so I could tell others about His most important Heavenly Book, The Book of Life!

I have a question for you. Where is your name written? Is it in the Book of Life, or could it be written in some book in hell waiting for you? My friends, before you die, you need to get your name in the Book of Life because: **CHAMPIONS MAKE SURE THEIR NAME IS IN THE BOOK OF LIFE**

IS IT TIME TO CHECK OUT?

It is about this time in the discussion that some people start to check out mentally. I work with ministries that go into prisons. When I do a basketball show in the prisons, the prisoners line up by the hundreds to watch the cool basketball tricks or to watch me ride my ten foot unicycle. The minute I start speaking about Jesus, some will start to walk away. You see, Jesus said that this

would happen. He said that if people rejected Him they will reject His followers as well. When people walk away, they are basically fulfilling Scripture. It says in Scripture: **"For the message of the cross is foolishness to those who are perishing, but to us who are being saved it is the power of God" (1 Cor. 1:10).**

JESUS NEVER BEGS HIS FOLLOWERS

Jesus never begged anyone to follow Him. For 2000 years, His message in the Bible has not changed, for He says to everyone, "Come follow me." We did not write this book to beg people to follow Christ because if we have to beg someone to follow Christ, people will have to beg them to go to church, or beg them to read a Bible, or beg them to pray. As a matter of fact, there is a cost to following Christ. When you follow Christ, you are actually promised 4 things: persecutions, trials, tribulations, and eternal life. The last one makes the first three all worth it. Jesus didn't say it would be easy, but I am here to tell you that it is worth it!

HOW CAN WE BE SURE?

Now just wait a second, you say. This all sounds interesting, but how can we be sure that the God of the Bible is the TRUE God, and that the Bible is the TRUE book? Not everybody can be right.

You are correct, for there are a lot of other religions out there, right? Maybe the Muslims have it right, and Allah is the true God, and the Koran is the true book. Or maybe it is Buddha. Could it be Confucius, or maybe it is one of the gods of the Hindus? Or better yet, maybe the Humanists have it right, and man is god? Maybe the atheists have it right, and there is no God. These are relevant issues that bring up three questions: 1) **Is there a God?** And if there is, 2) **Who is He?** And 3) **What does He require?**

IS THERE A GOD?

How do we really know that there is a God? There are many in today's world who don't believe in God. Can all these people be wrong? If you are an atheist and don't believe in God, I have news for you. According to Romans chapter one, the existence of God is apparent from the works of creation, so you are without excuse.

If the existence of God is so apparent, why would a person not believe that there is a God? It is really simple, because they have been brainwashed into thinking that there isn't a God and they don't even realize it.

WHAT IS BRAINWASHING?

BRAINWASHING – a forcible indoctrination to induce someone to give up basic political, social, or religious beliefs and attitudes and to accept contrasting ideas

Marian Webster Dictionary (m-w.com)

For most Americans, we didn't have a choice. The world's agenda was forced upon us. This brainwashing started when we were very young. In public school in the first grade we were told that we are on the earth because of a cosmic burp that happened billions and billions of years ago. We are the product of evolution (EVIL–lution), the lie that says that you went from the GOO, to the ZOO, to YOU!

This lie was reinforced all the way through grade school. In high school, we found out that God no longer fits into the world's equation anymore. By the time we went to college, we were fortunate if we believed in God, because we had been convinced that God was just a silly idea invented by weak people, and the Bible was just an outdated fairy tale. God had been replaced by science. Even if we believed in God, we were outnumbered by all our brainwashed friends and peers who heard the same propaganda and now believed the lie.

If I showed you my computer, and I told you

that over the course of many years a wind storm threw together a bunch of plastic, silicon, and metal parts and made my working computer. Would you believe me? NO, you wouldn't! Why? Because a computer has precise design, and is a sophisticated creation. A wind storm of random chance could not place everything in the correct order because a computer has order and exquisite design. Your body and your brain are a billion times more sophisticated than a silly computer. Scripture tells us in Psalms 139:14 you are: **"... fearfully and wonderfully made..."** When God made you, He made you unique, with unfathomable design and abilities!

Here is an illustration comparing the brain of the honeybee with the Cray Super Computer. This analogy is taken from *Creation Science Video* by Dr. Kent Hovind.

CRAY Supercomputer vs. Honyebee		
Size:	Huge	Tiny
Speed:	6 billion/sec	1 trillion/sec
Energy Used:	10 million k-watts	1 Microwatt
Cost:	$48,000,000+	Cheap
Maintenance:	Many people	none (self healing)
Weight:	2300 lbs	Not Much
Conclusions:	Designed	Evolved??

From Creation Science - Dr. Kent Hovind

The most incredible thing is, the human brain is millions of times more complex than a honeybee's! Dr. Isaac Asimov said, **"And in man is a three-pound brain, which, as far as we know, is the most complex and orderly arrangement of matter in the universe."**
Dr. Isaac Asimov, Smithsonian Journal; June, 1970, P. 10-11

To believe that there is not a God is a very foolish

thing indeed, for the proof that there is a God is found in Scripture: **"The heavens declare the glory of God; and the firmament shows His handy work" (Ps. 19:1).**

There is an illustration that goes like this: Where you see a painting, you have a painter, and where you see a building, you have a builder. You don't have to meet the painter, or the builder to know that these people exist. Their painting and their building speak of their existence. In the same way, where you have a creation, you know that there is a creator. The proof of the existence of God is all around you. Better yet, go look in the mirror! You will see all the proof you need! By sheer logic, you would have to be a fool to believe that there isn't a God, for creation is screaming it out!

If you don't believe in God, the world calls you an atheist but in the Bible, God also has a name for you as well. He calls you a FOOL! Psalms 14:1 says: **"The fool says in his heart, 'there is no God'"**. Why would God call you a fool? Because creation screams out the existence of God. So, for those atheists who say they don't believe in God. Remember. God believes in YOU! And He loves YOU! Christians are called people of faith, but to be an atheist, it takes even more faith than believing in God. **You have to believe that NO ONE, TIMES NOTHING, PLUS BLIND CHANCE, EQUALS EVERYTHING. That my friend, takes a lot of faith!**

Either the atheist is right, and there isn't a God; or the believer is right, and there is a God. **If the atheist is right we have nothing to lose. BUT if those who believe in God are right, then those who don't believe in God have everything to lose!**

WHO IS HE?

Now that we have logically determined that there is a God. We come to the next question: Who is He? Could it be Allah? Or is it Buddha? Or is it one of the Hindu gods? Or is it a no-named higher power? Or is it

man? Or could it really be Jesus? Let's check it out.

Ray Comfort, at Livingwaters.com, has some of the best Gospel Tracts and information on how to share your faith. In his book and his video series called, *Hell's Best Kept Secret*, he gives an excellent illustration about a parachute. We have paraphrased and modified that illustration for this book:

THE GIFT OF A PARACHUTE

Imagine that you were offered a choice of five gifts:

1) The original *Mona Lisa* painting;
2) The keys to a brand new Lamborghini;
3) A million dollars in cash;
4) A person to teach you how to flap your arms
5) A parachute

You can pick only one. Which would you choose? Before you decide, here is some crucial information about your predicament that will help you make the wisest choice:

You are about to jump 10,000 feet out of an airplane. Does that little piece of information help you with your decision? It should because you need the parachute. It's the only one of the five gifts that will help with your dilemma. The others may have some value, but they are useless when it comes to facing the law of gravity in a 10,000-foot fall.

NOW THINK OF THE FIVE MAJOR RELIGIONS

1) Hinduism
2) Buddhism
3) Islam
4) Humanism
5) Christianity

Which one should you choose? Before you decide which religion, here's some information that will help you determine which one is the wisest choice:

All of humanity stands on the edge of eternity. Each of us will have to jump through a door called death. It could happen to us in fifty years or in two years or today. For most of humanity, death is a huge and terrifying plummet into the unknown. So what should we do? We will have to face the Law of Sin and Death. Which of the major religions will help us in our predicament? Concerning the major religions, here is an interesting quote:

> Buddha never claimed to be God.
> Moses never claimed to be Jehovah.
> Mohammed never claimed to be Allah.
> Yet Jesus Christ claimed to be the true and living God.
> Buddha simply said, "I am a teacher in search of the Truth."
> Jesus said, "I am the truth."
> Confucius said, "I never claimed to be holy."
> Jesus said, "Who convicts me of sin?"
> Mohammed said, "Unless God throws his cloak of mercy over me, I have no hope."
> Jesus said: "Unless you believe in me, you will die in your sins."
> Author unknown

CONVERT OR ELSE!

There are some religions who claim to have the truth and will go to great lengths to force people to believe. Some will threaten to excommunicate you from family and friends and will even try to kill you if you don't convert! These religions use hatred and fear. That doesn't sound too loving. I think I will pass on those religions, and you would be wise to do the same.

WHAT ABOUT MAN?

Maybe Humanism is right and man is the answer. After all, we have been told that man is evolving into a godlike state, right? Maybe man is the one who needs to be honored and worshiped? Hmmmm, let's see. Looking at the depravity that we see in people, from the lowest to the highest members of our society, I will venture to say, "Sorry, but I don't think so!"

What does the Bible say about man? According to Jeremiah 17:9, the heart of man is not only wicked, it is desperately wicked.

The middle verse of the whole Bible is also in the middle chapter of the whole Bible. That verse is Psalms 118:8 it says: **"Do not put your trust in man, but put your trust in God."** If God placed that verse in the very middle of the Bible, He has an important message for us. Don't you think? The message is this: Don't trust in man! That sounds like good advice.

AS LONG AS YOU BELIEVE IN SOMETHING

There are many people in today's society that believe in a higher power and as long as you believe in something, that is good enough. They believe that all religions are basically saying the same thing, therefore all roads lead to heaven. According to Jesus, all religions do not lead to heaven, and are not saying the same thing. Jesus said in John 14:6, **"I am the way, the truth, and the life. No one comes to the Father except through Me."** Either Jesus is right and is who He claims to be, or He is wrong and is the biggest deceiver of all time! We need to decide quickly because the jump is coming.

CHRISTIANITY IS DIFFERENT

So what makes Christianity so different? Personally, I do not consider true Christianity to be a religion. Christianity is not a religion but rather a relationship with the Living God. Religion is man's attempt to reach God, but Christianity is God reaching down to sinful man through Jesus Christ His Son.

WHAT SETS JESUS APART?

How is Jesus different from His so-called competition? Let's start with the book that talks about Him, the Bible. That book is the best selling, most widely distributed, most read book in the history of mankind. There is not even a close second. Over six billion Bibles have been either given away or sold from the time Bibles have been printed up until 1975. With the advent of computer technology, ebook readers, and modern printing presses, today those numbers are staggering. The Bible has been translated into 1200 languages, more than any other book. It is also the most stolen book in history. The Bible claims to be divinely inspired with the theme of God's creation of man, the fall of man and the redemption of man through Jesus Christ, the Son of God.

JESUS IS GOD IN THE FLESH

Concerning Jesus, He is the main subject of this best selling book! Not including the Bible, more books and songs have been written about and dedicated to this man than any other figure in history, dead or alive. When He came to earth, HE LITERALLY SPLIT TIME! We date our modern calendar by His birth, death, and resurrection. More people want to follow Him not because they have to, like some religions, but because they want to! The influence and scope of Jesus crosses age, race, and language barriers.

> "The power of Christ knows no boundary of time or space. In our own age, many skeptics have been convinced just as thoroughly as their first-century counterparts. For example, Lew Wallace, a famous general and literary genius was a known atheist. For two years, Wallace studied in the leading libraries of Europe and America, seeking information that would forever

destroy Christianity. While writing the second chapter of a book outlining his arguments, he suddenly found himself on his knees crying out to Jesus, 'My Lord and my God.' When confronted by solid indisputable evidence, he could no longer deny that Jesus Christ was the Son of God. Later, Lew Wallace wrote the book Ben Hur, one of the greatest English novels ever written concerning the time of Christ."

http://www.whoisjesus-really.com/english/impact.htm

When you read the Gospels, you will see that Jesus made fantastic claims that have stood the test of time. No other person but God could back up the claims He made. He came to earth and claimed to be God in the flesh fulfilling many Old Testament Scriptures. He backed up His claims about being God in the flesh by answering His critics with profound wisdom like no other could. He taught people how to live, give, lead, serve, and mostly how to love. His humility and His teachings were so profound that it set Him apart from every person who ever walked this earth. Armies have tried conquering men, but throughout history, Jesus Christ has conquered more men than any country, religious figure, or army. He did not do it with swords, guns, spears, deception, fear, hatred, or the threat of death. He did it through one word. That word is LOVE!

If that wasn't enough, He backed up His teachings by miracles. In the Gospels, He healed sick people; cripples could walk, lepers were cleansed, deaf could hear, blind could see, and He even raised people from the dead.

The miracles weren't just with people but also with nature. He changed water to wine; He took a few fish and a little bread and fed a multitude; He walked on water; He calmed storms; He had his disciple Peter catch a fish, which by sheer chance, had a coin in its mouth so that He could pay his taxes; and He cast devils out of people. To top it off, He predicted that He would suffer and die on a cross, but would rise again three days later. It all came to pass just as he predicted!

Jesus claimed to get to the root of man's problems by defeating man's three greatest enemies: sin, the devil, and death. They were defeated at the cross. The twelve apostles who walked with Him, along with many others, believed that Jesus was who He claimed to be to the point of giving their whole lives for Him and then suffering or dying for Him.

Of all of these great things mentioned, the thing that really sets Jesus apart from the rest of His so called competition is His greatest miracle of all, HIS LOVE! He truly loved people unconditionally. Most people will only love when it is convenient, but Jesus gave us a new concept that was called unconditional love! Romans 5:8 says, **"But God demonstrates His own love toward us, in that while we were still sinners, Christ died for us."** This is a love that says no matter what you have done to me, I am still going to love YOU!

Old people, young people, and children all experienced His love! He loved sinners: adulterers, criminals, and thieves! The love didn't stop there, for He even loved His enemies! While Jesus was hanging on the cross, He proved His love for His enemies. What did Jesus do? He prayed for them! He said: **"Father, forgive them, for they know not what they are doing" (Luke 23:34).** Right before He died He was still loving people!

It is the Love of God expressed through His believers that draws people to Christ. Today, God shows His love by revealing to us our true state. What is our true condition? The Ten Commandments show us what it is. If you don't know the commandments, we have drawn them up in picture form for ease of memory. See chart illustration on this page.

THE LAW OF SIN & DEATH

After we die we have to face what is called "the law of sin and death" (see Romans 8:2). Most people know that Law as "The Ten Commandments". It says in Psalms 19:7, **"The law of the Lord is perfect, converting the soul."** Did God give us the commandments as a way to get to heaven? No, He gave them to us as a way to convert our souls. The commandments are a moral mirror to look at. When we look at God's laws; they reveal a problem. What is the problem? We don't measure up to God's perfection. We are sinful and in need of a Savior.

But there are some that will say, "Yes, I have broken a few of commandments, but there are a lot of people who are worse than me, besides I have done a lot of good things, too!"

According to James 2:10, that logic will not work: **"For whoever shall keep the whole law, and yet stumble in one point, he is guilty of all."** It doesn't matter if you have broken just one commandment, according to this verse, breaking one makes us guilty of breaking them all.

Some people think that even if they have broken God's commandments they can make up for it by good works. Ephesians 2:8-9 says: **"For by grace you have been saved through faith, and that not of yourselves**

it is the gift of God, not of works lest anyone should boast." Salvation is a GIFT freely given by the giver. It does not require church membership, money, position, power, or good works. In Isaiah 64:6, God calls our good works **"Filthy rags"**. Think of the best thing you can do for God. Did you know that to Him, it looks like a filthy rag. According to that verse in Ephesians, the only thing that is required is faith in Jesus Christ.

What is Faith? Faith is like believing, only greater. It is belief with trust. Trying to get to heaven by being a good person is like jumping out of the plane and flapping your arms. It might be a good effort, but you will hit the ground going 150 mph! God loves us so much that He shows us what we really are, sinners in need of a savior.

INNOCENT OR GUILTY?
If we were standing before God today, would we be innocent or guilty of breaking His commandments? If we are honest, we would have to say guilty. According to the Bible, if we are guilty, would we go to Heaven or Hell? Without Jesus, we are all going to Hell. That is the bad news. **But we didn't write this book to give you bad news, we wrote it to give you the good news, Jesus came to set you FREE!**

ARE YOU READY TO JUMP?
Now imagine you are in the plane standing at the edge of that 10,000-foot drop. You realize that you have to jump. Then someone offers you the original *Mona Lisa*. You throw it aside. Another person hands you the keys to a brand new Lamborghini. You let them drop to the floor. Someone else tries to put a million dollars into your hands. You push the person's hand away. Someone offers to show you the best way to flap your arms, and you start to cry because you know it is a hopeless cause! Suddenly, you hear a voice say, "Do you want a parachute?" Which one of those five people is going to

hold the most credibility in your eyes? Of course, it is the one who held up the parachute because it is the answer to your problem!

In Christianity, God Himself provided a "parachute" for the real problem confronting man. What is the problem? Judgment is coming, and at death we will be forced to jump into the unknown. How did God solve our dilemma? He satisfied God's judgment by becoming a man and taking our punishment upon Himself. In Second Corinthians 5, Scripture tells us that God was in Christ reconciling the world to Himself.

God's Word says to **"Put on the Lord Jesus Christ" (Romans 13:14)**. If we don't have the parachute of the Lord Jesus when we jump through the door of death, we will be judged guilty and face the consequences of the law of sin and death. Just as we put on a parachute to save us from the Law of Gravity, so we need to put on the Lord Jesus Christ to save us from the consequences of the Law of Sin and Death.

God loves you so much that He became a sinless human being in the person of Jesus Christ of Nazareth. The Savior died an excruciating death on the cross and took the punishment that we deserved upon Himself. **"Christ has redeemed us from the curse of the law, being made a curse for us" (Galatians 3:13)**. We broke the Law, but He became a man to pay our penalty by shedding His blood. Now God can forgive every sin you have ever committed, so you no longer need to be tormented by the fear of death. God has provided you a parachute and the choice is up to you! What do we do now? I know what you need to do----Become a Champion and get your name in God's Book!

WHAT DOES GOD REQUIRE?

God requires for you to get your name in the Book of Life! To do this, there are some things you must do. The first message that Jesus preached is found in the Gospel of Matthew, where He said these words: "... **Repent, for the kingdom of heaven is at hand" (Matthew 3:2).** The word repent, means to turn from your sins and turn toward God. This requires a change of attitude and a change of heart.

According to Romans 10:9, there are two requirements to get your name into God's Book of Life. It says, **"that if you confess with your mouth the Lord Jesus and believe in your heart that God has raised Him from the dead, you will be saved."** Step one, confess with your mouth and step two, believe in your heart. I have met a lot of people who are willing to confess Christ, but their hearts are far from God. God doesn't want your lips, He wants your heart. In a few moments, we are going to give you an opportunity to give your life to Christ. But if your heart isn't in it shut this book right now, and don't pray, for it won't mean a thing to you, and it certainly will not mean a thing to God. If you know you have broken God's laws, and you have no idea where your name is written, then today is your day. God has a gift for you that you can receive by faith, through prayer. If you are reading this and you are over the age of 14, I have some bad news for you.

BAD NEWS FOR ADULTS

If I lined up ten adult Christians and asked them, "How old were you when you came to faith in Jesus Christ?" Eight out of ten of them would say BEFORE the age of 14. (See Chart) Only two out of ten make commitments after the age of 14. If you are reading this book, you are over the age of 14, and you do not know the Lord, it may be more difficult for you to find Him.

There are basically three reasons for this: Fear, pride, and the love of the world. **Fear** -- you are too afraid of what other people are thinking. **Pride** – you are thinking of yourself more highly than you should. **Love of the world** – the cares and the riches of the world are choking

out God and are producing Ego in your life. Ego is spelled E – G – O, and that stands for Edging God Out. God has been edged out of your life because of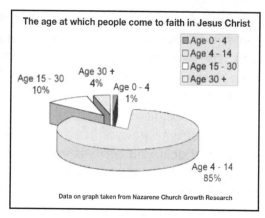
Fear, Pride and Love of the world. If you don't know the Lord, I have a challenge for you. Swallow your Fear, Swallow your Pride, and Swallow your Love of the world and for a few minutes let God work in your heart.

HOW BIG IS THE DOORWAY TO HEAVEN?

Jesus said, **"Assuredly, I say to you, unless you are converted and become as little children, you will by no means enter the kingdom of heaven"** (Matthew 18:3).

Did you know that the doorway to heaven is figuratively only three feet tall. Little children fit with ease. But if you are over three feet tall, the only way you are going to fit is on bended knee. In other words, you have to humble yourself before God, admit to God that you have broken His commandments and are in need of a savior. If you do, God will save your soul.

GET RIGHT WITH GOD TODAY

My friend, when you are standing at death's door and you will stand there someday, there is only one who will be able to help you at that moment. His name is Jesus! God has a place for you in His Book of Life. God has done everything needed to save you from Hell, but the decision is up to you! It says in John, 3:3, "Jesus answered, **'Most assuredly, I say to you, unless one is born again, he cannot see the kingdom of God.'"**

Are you born again into God's kingdom? If you have been born once in this world, (Physical birth) I have bad news, you will die twice. (Physical and spiritual death) If you have been born twice in this world, (Physical and spiritual birth) you will only die once. The rest is eternal life through Jesus Christ our Lord.

You don't know when you will take that leap through the door of death, but you need the parachute of Jesus Christ to save you! Pray to him right now and ask God to make you Born Again! Confess your sins to God, put your trust in Jesus to save you, and you will pass from death to life. You have God's promise on it (See John 5:24). Pray something like this:

Dear Heavenly Father, I confess to you that I have broken your commandments, and I do not deserve Heaven. Today, I turn away from all of my sins (name them). I put my trust in Jesus Christ alone as my Lord and Savior. Please forgive me, change my heart, and grant me Your gift of everlasting life. Please write my name in your Book of Life, and help me be a Champion for You! In Jesus' name I pray. Amen.

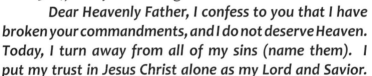

We have great news for you! If you prayed from your heart, asked Jesus to forgive you, and repented of your sins, CONGRATULATIONS! WE ARE BROTHERS AND SISTERS IN CHRIST! It says in Second Corinthians 5:17: **"Therefore, if anyone is in Christ, he is a new creation; old things have passed away; behold, all things have become new"** (2 Corinthians 5:17).

THANK YOU TANYA

CODE #2
CHAMPIONS GET TO KNOW JESUS CHRIST

"Now this is eternal life: that they know you, the only true God, and Jesus Christ, whom you have sent" (John 17:3).

"Whoever does not love does not know God, because God is love" (1 John 4:8).

STORY:
BREAKING IN THE NEW YEAR

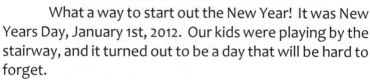

What a way to start out the New Year! It was New Years Day, January 1st, 2012. Our kids were playing by the stairway, and it turned out to be a day that will be hard to forget.

"Tessa come down from there." Twelve year old Ben said to three year old Tessa as she climbed on top of our stairway railing.

"Ben, you can catch me!" Tessa said.

"Tessa don't do it! That's not safe!" Ben said as Tessa jumped at Ben.

As Tessa leaped, she slipped and headed toward Ben, but she came up short, hit the step and twisted her leg.

About 5 minutes later, Josiah came out to get me in the shed.

"Dad, Tessa's leg really hurts, and she is crying in the house. Mom sent me out here to get you, because she wants you to come in and check it out." Josiah said with a concerned look on his face.

"What happened, Josiah? Is she OK?"

"I guess she was on the railing of our stairway and just jumped. As she hit the step, she kind of twisted her leg," he explained.

We headed into the house and there was Diane with Tessa. Diane was trying to comfort our little twin as she was laying on the table. Tessa was sniffling as she laid there and right next to her was her best little buddy, her identical twin, Tori.

"Tessa, are you OK?" I said as I tried to pick up her left leg.

"Ouch, daddy, that really hurts!" Tessa said as she flinched with her body and started to cry.

She was in a lot of pain and it was hurting her upper thigh. Every time someone would move her or her leg, she gave out a scream.

"Do you think it might be a pulled muscle or a sprain," Diane asked as we both tried to diagnose the problem.

"I don't know," I said as we held her hand and tried not to move her much.

But the more we waited, we noticed the pain wasn't subsiding, and her upper leg was swelling. So we decided to take her into the local clinic and have it x-rayed.

As we brought her in, the nurse asked how she hurt it and Tessa, through her tears, tried to explain to them what she did. The nurse assured us that little kids' bones are pretty flexible. It was most likely not broken but to be on the safe side they x-rayed her upper left thigh.

About one half hour later, the doctor came into our waiting room, and gave us the news.

"Well, I didn't think she broke it, but she did! She has a clean break, a spiral fracture on her femur bone on the left thigh!" The doctor explained as he pulled up the x-ray on the computer.

"I guess I am pretty surprised that she broke it, for that doesn't happen too often. She must have hit it just right," The doctor said as we all looked at the x-ray.

"Wow, that is quite a break," I said.

"Yes, I am glad that we brought her in," Diane said.

"Where do we go from here?" I asked.

"Because it is a clean break, the muscles have pulled the bones too far up so we will have to put her in traction with a 3 pound weight on her leg. Over the course of the next 3 days, this will cause those muscles

to relax and will pull the bones apart so that we can cast it so the leg will heal to the correct length." The doctor explained.

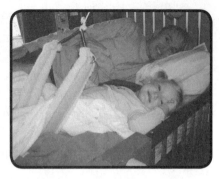

So we prepared for a hospital stay, and over the next 3 days, we tried to comfort little Tessa in her agony. It was a difficult time for everyone involved, but it was especially a tough time for our three year old little girl, and her twin sister, Tori. Those two had never been apart from each other since they were born. While Diane and I were in the hospital with Tessa, Tessa was missing Tori, and Tori was certainly missing Tessa. Not only was it tough being away from her best friend, but the leg was painful as well. She cried intermittently throughout the days and nights, and you could tell it was a trying time for Tessa.

We were getting reports from home and would call often to let Tori talk to Tessa on the phone while she had her leg strapped in the traction device.

"Tessa, the phone is for your. It is Tori, she is really missing you." Diane said as she handed the phone to Tessa.

"Hello, Tessa? This is Tori. Are you OK? Did you hurt your leg? Can I come and see you?" Asked Tori.

"Yes Tori, I hurt my leg, and I wish you could come and see me," Tessa said as she started to cry.

Diane and I spent most of the time, sitting or standing by her bedside holding her hand. She got brief moments of sleep, and so many times we wished we could take some of the pain away.

Because she couldn't move, the hours would just drag on for little Tessa. On the second day in the hospital, she was crying some real tears. When she did, I grabbed her hand and placed my other hand behind her little head and rubbed the back of her neck. I couldn't help but shed a few tears with my little girl. When she saw me crying, it made her cry even more to the point she was choking it back. She then leaned her little face toward mine and said, "Daddy, I am sorry for breaking my femur."

Wow, that statement melted my heart and to see her blaming herself for the situation was very difficult.

"It's OK, Tessa. We will get through this with God's strength. We are praying that God is going to heal you so you are good as new," I said as I tried to comfort both her and me.

"Thank you, Daddy."

While we were there with Tessa, Diane and I had time to think and reflect. Diane and I had a flashback.

"Hey Diane, what does this remind you of?" I said as we were comforting little Tessa.

"It reminds me of sitting in the hospital with Isaiah and Josiah. Even though Tessa is suffering here, those situations with those two boys were life threatening. I am just thankful to the Lord to be on the other side of those days," she responded.

"Me, too!"

When you have kids, things can happen that can be out of your control. In 1991, when our third son, Isaiah, was just six months old, he got really sick and had to be airlifted to the hospital. He came down with what we thought was the flu, but it didn't go away and because of it he ended up having a febrile seizure. The doctors diagnosed it as Spinal Meningitis and gave us a very grim prognosis. They said that if Isaiah lived, he was going to be blind, deaf or mentally retarded because of lack of oxygen to the brain.

Bruce & Diane with one month old Josiah!

Five years later, we were back again with our fifth son, Josiah, who was only one month old. He was just a little guy, and we ended up in the hospital with him with a bad case of pneumonia. We about lost him. In both cases, the doctors told us that if the boys were to live, there were going to be problems.

I have had different things happen to me where I had to suffer some physical affliction, but to see your own flesh and blood, a helpless little baby, fighting for life brings a whole new meaning to the word suffering. In both cases, there was nothing we could do but pray to the One who holds the keys to life and death. We figured that if God can create the universe then something as little as healing a baby should be nothing for Him. To be honest, I didn't feel like we had enough faith for God to work out our situation. When you are in the trenches going through the battle, it is so tough not to let the fear of the circumstances get the best of you. The only thing we could do, was pray!

Pray we did. We asked God to raise them up, and that they would be back to normal. In both cases, we prayed for them in the Name of Jesus and anointed them with oil like it says in the Bible in James chapter five. In both instances, the doctors were shocked at the improvement! The Great Physician came through!

As I write, both boys pulled out of it and have grown into fine young men. Today, we are happy to report that both Isaiah and Josiah are totally normal. Oh, about the brain damage for Isaiah. He graduated Magna Cum Laude from South Dakota State University and is now in his second year of Chiropractic College. Josiah recently graduated from High School and is studying for his Real Estate License. God reminded us that He is the one pulling the strings, and He can and will come through when we need Him!

Back to Tessa:

On the third day of being in traction, the doctor and three nurses took her off traction and into another room to put a cast on her. For Tessa, I could tell it was the most painful part of the whole process.

When they brought her out from the casting room, we saw her cast and the cast was shocking to say the least! It started at the bottom of her left foot; went up her whole left leg; wrapped around her waist; and proceeded to go halfway down her right leg. Her legs were slightly spread and she was cast in the seated bent leg position. The cast was very large and cumbersome, and it was one of those unbelievable looking casts that you would see in a medical book for someone who had been in a very bad accident.

After they put the cast on, the nurses checked Tessa and the cast over and made adjustments here and there. Then they tried to explain to Diane and I the best mode of making it all work. There was a small opening in the bottom of the cast for her to go to the bathroom, but the whole thing was rather shocking to say the least. The cast didn't seem to help her with pain, for she seemed to be in more pain than before. Now you could hardly move

her without a shrieking cry of agony.

"Wow, that is quite a cast", Diane said as we talked with the doctor.

"Yes, in order for that upper thigh bone, the femur, to heal properly, it has to be immobile. This is the only type of cast that will work in this situation." The doctor explained.

"How long does the cast have to be on?" Diane asked as we started gathering our stuff from the hospital room.

"We will check the progress about once a week, but she is going to have to wear it for about 8 weeks," The doctor said as Diane and I tried to take it all in.

We got our stuff together, and I was trying to pick up Tessa to carry her out to the car. She was in so much pain that even the slightest movement would send her screaming. We eventually just put her on a flat board with pillows under her legs and carried her out on the board to the car. We kept her on it until we got home, and this seemed to help her so that she didn't have to bend at the waist.

She was crying intermittently on the trip home, and after we got her home we were trying to figure out how to manage Tessa without moving her much. It became a twenty four-hour day ordeal with dressing her, bathing her, taking her to the bathroom, and comforting her all through the night during this painful ordeal. Even though she was so tired, it was very hard for her to sleep. Because the cast was so cumbersome when she did sleep it was only for a few minutes at time.

The whole situation reminded me of a game that we played at home, called Bandu. The game consists of odd shaped wooden blocks such as squares, cylinders, round balls, and even one wooden block that looks like an egg. The object of the game is that each player has to build a stack of blocks on top of one small rectangular platform. What makes the game interesting is that other people get to choose what pieces you get. After they give you a certain shaped block, you have to stack what you get on top of that small rectangular platform or on top of other blocks that are already there.

The person who can stack the most without their tower falling wins. What makes the game difficult is that you don't know what piece you are going to have to stack. The pieces that are most desirable are the square ones that look like bricks for they are the easiest to stack. One of the most undesirable pieces is the wooden egg. It is hard to stack it on anything and even harder to stack anything on top of it.

This whole situation with Tessa's broken leg reminded me of getting that egg in the game of Bandu. It just didn't fit anywhere! We were trying to figure out how to stack this unstackable piece, but it wasn't fitting into our world. We prayed and asked God to give strength to Tessa to deal with the pain, for the wisdom to figure it all out, and for the patience to endure it.

As always, God was coming through. Lifting and handling Tessa was just so awkward. Any movement was very painful for her. On the first night as I lay there in bed, I thought about that board that we brought her home on. When she was laying on the board with her legs on a pillow, she was more comfortable because she didn't have to bend. God gave me an idea on how to minimize the bending of

her body.

The next day I went out to our workshop and built her a little custom made chair that had wheels on it. This little chair was like a wheelchair that had swivel wheels on the bottom. But this chair was unique in that it had a removable seat portion with handles on it. The seat could be on the wheels or we could detach it with Tessa strapped onto it. This kept her body from bending, and she could actually stay in the seat portion of the chair all the time. It was like putting a handle on a child. This made it easy to take to her to the bathroom or to bed. It minimized the bending and the pain, which made her life and our life more manageable.

We also built and designed a little removable bucket on the bottom of the seat so she could actually go potty on the seat while it was attached to the wheels. This made the bathroom breaks a little easier as well.

When the removable seat was on the wheels, Tessa could be pushed around by her brothers and sisters. We even made her a removable tray table so she could eat, play and draw pictures.

The little chair became so popular around the house that Tori said, "Daddy, could I break my leg, too? I want you to make me a chair like Tessa's."

"Believe me, Tori, you don't want your leg to break! One of those is enough. I tell you what, when Tessa is in the chair we will try to make room for you, and you can sit on it with her," I said.

"That sounds fun!" Tori said with a smile!

The little chair was not only popular at home but also at the clinic for our weekly doctor visits! When we took Tessa in for her checkup, our doctor was impressed with the design and thought I should sell the idea to some medical company.

After about a month of riding in the chair 24/7, Tessa was slowly getting better. Her leg was slowly on the mend and was hurting less. Because she was getting used to the cumbersome cast, she was becoming more mobile. At first, she started crawling with her arms while dragging her casted legs behind her. She was getting around quite well. She got to the point where she would drag herself up to a table or couch, and could stand up in the cast.

Then she did something I didn't think was possible. For the last week in the cast, she was walking around the house in it! It was so hilarious to watch her walk in this cumbersome cast. When she would walk, the bottom of her casted foot would hit the floor and had a "clop" sound.

After two months, the x-rays were showing the bones were knitting back together and the gaps between the break were slowly disappearing. We then scheduled an appointment for Tessa to have the cast removed. The cast was so large that when the doctors were cutting it off, and pealing it back, it was almost as if Tessa was being hatched out of an egg! The first thing she did was itch and itch and itch her left leg!

"Oh, mommy, that feels so good to have the cast off," Tessa said as she spent the next five minutes itching her leg and asking her mom to itch it as well.

"We are so glad that you are getting the cast off!" Diane said.

We headed home. Because her leg was so weak, Tessa walked with a limp for the next month. But each week, she slowly made improvements.

Now the whole broken femur situation is a distant memory for Tessa and us in the school of hard knocks. The doctors and nurses did a great job, and the leg healed up beautifully. Six months after it happened,

61

Tessa was running, jumping, and playing like nothing ever happened. Today, Tessa is totally back to normal, and we are grateful to God for answering our prayers.

APPLICATION: CHAMPIONS GET TO KNOW JESUS CHRIST

While we were sitting in the hospital with Tessa, God the Father gave me a revelation that has to do with Code Number Two.

After a person makes a commitment to Christ, there becomes a desire to not just know the facts about Jesus, but to get know Him personally as a friend. Who is this God that loved me so much, that He came to earth to die for me? This all consuming love will not only move your heart, it will change our heart forever!

John 17:3 says it all and shares what we are going to be doing for all eternity. We are going to get to know God. **"Now this is eternal life: that they know you, the only true God, and Jesus Christ, whom you have sent."**

While Diane and I were sitting in the hospital and almost lost both Isaiah in 1991, and Josiah in 1996; and with Tessa's leg in 2012, God gave us a revelation of His love, and a small taste of what God the Father went through when he saw His Son Jesus, suffering in the grip of sinful man. God our Father sat back in agony and watched them not only torture His Son but kill Him as well! To know God the Father and His Son Jesus is to know what they went through for us. God wants us to fellowship in His sufferings, because it is through sufferings that true love is exhibited. You can say you love someone all you want, but it is all talk until you sacrifice and suffer for that person. In Romans 5:8 God proved His love for us, in that while we were still sinners, Christ died for us. God's love was proved through His suffering.

Paul had it figured out as well. He says in Philippians

3:10-11: *"... that I may know Him and the power of His resurrection, <u>and the fellowship of His sufferings</u>, being conformed to His death, if by any means, I may attain to the resurrection from the dead."* (Emphasis mine)

YOU WILL NEVER HAVE THIS CHANCE AGAIN

When we stand before Christ at the judgment, it will be easy to want to know Him because we will be consumed by His love, radiance, and glory. We will all fall flat on our face in fear and terror at the sight of the living God! At that moment, the King of Kings and the Lord of Lords will be before us in all of His Majesty.

While we are on the earth, God has given us a once in an eternity opportunity! We will never get this chance again! That is the opportunity, to get to know Jesus Christ without being able to see Him. To Love Him, Worship Him, Honor Him, and TO SUFFER FOR HIM while He hides His glory from us. In Heaven, there will be no suffering. True love is showed through sacrifice and suffering. Because we can't see Him as He is, it takes faith. What exactly is faith? We have the definition in **Hebrews 11:1, "Now faith is the substance of things hoped for, the evidence of things not seen."** We have the evidence of God's power all around us. What will we do with that evidence? Live for ourselves, or by faith get to know the one who makes it all happen and live for Him.

LISTENING FOR THE VOICE OF GOD

To know God, you must listen for His voice. John 10:27 says, **"My sheep hear My voice, and I know them, and they follow me."**

Throughout the Scriptures, God spoke to His children in many ways. He speaks to us through His Word, the Bible. He speaks to us through others. He speaks to us through an actual audible voice or through dreams and visions. But in my experience, most of the

time, God speaks through a still small voice. For me it was the same voice that I heard in my mind that brought me to Him in the first place.

If your heart's desire is to love and obey God, it isn't complicated to hear His voice. If you want to hear God's voice, these four steps will put you in the proper attitude to hear Him:

1) **Worship the Lord and confess all sin.** (Ps. 66:18) Worship the Lord daily for a meaningful period of time, and pray continuously throughout the day. Ask Him for the answer to your question.

2) **Submit to His Lordship.** Ask Him to quiet all the worldly thoughts, desires, and voices of others. Shut off the TV, radio, computer, video games, i-pod, etc., so that you heart can hear God. (2 Cor. 10:5)

3) **Resist the enemy.** (James 4:7-8) Ask the Lord for discernment so the devil will not deceive you. God will never give you an answer contrary to His Word or His nature.

4) **Be consistent and expect an answer from God.** God may give you an answer through the Scriptures. He may bring someone into your life who will give you an answer from the Lord. He may use some circumstance in your life as the answer. He may give you a dream or a vision. Or God will speak to you through the still small voice. Just as you can recognize the voice of a family member on the phone, as you consistently listen for God's voice, you will recognize it. If you are to consumed by worldly things like listening to your i-pod, watch TV, or video games, you will never be able to hear His voice. As Psalms 46:10 says, **"Be still, and know that I am God;..."**

ONLY DEAD MEN CAN SEE GOD

In the Old Testament, Moses was an example of a person who got to know God in a very personal way.

As a matter of fact, he knew God on a whole new level. When God spoke to Him, it was an incredible experience. Check out this Scripture: **"Since then there has not arisen in Israel a prophet like Moses, whom the Lord knew face to face" (Deut. 34:10).**

But how is this possible? For there is a Scripture where God says in Exodus, **"You cannot see My face; for no man shall see Me and live" (Exodus 33:20).** These two Scriptures almost seem to contradict one another. For one says that no man can see God and live, and the other one says that Moses talked with God face to face. Do they contradict? Can a person see God on this side of death?

As believers in Christ after we die, we will then have the opportunity to see God. But as I read the Scriptures, I noticed that there were examples where God would reveal Himself to certain men, and these men saw God, yet they didn't die. Along with Moses there are other examples. In Isaiah chapter six, Isaiah saw the Lord high and lifted up. In the book of Daniel, the three young men who didn't worship the idol were thrown into the fiery furnace. While in the furnace, there was One like the Son of God walking around with them in the fire. In the book of Acts, the apostle Paul was caught up to the third Heaven and lived to tell about the experience. John, on the isle of Patmos, was brought into the presence of the Lord and saw Jesus face to face and lived to tell about it. Is it possible that God will reveal Himself to believers who get to know Him while they inhabit their physical bodies?

The answer to the question may surprise you, as it is both yes and no. Yes, it is possible to see God on this side of death, and no it is not possible to do so and live, *because only dead men can see God.* If you notice the people who did see God and lived to share about the experience were people who were sold out for the things of God. Even though they were alive, **THEY WERE DEAD**

TO THEMSELVES AND TO THE THINGS OF THE WORLD! EVERY DAY, THEY DIED TO THE FLESH! YOU CAN CALL THEM "WALKING DEAD MEN". If you truly want to get to know the Lord on this level, you are going to have to die to the flesh and to the things of this world.

Some people have this impression that if they come to Christ that their problems will subside or disappear. That is not necessarily the case. God can and does help you through difficulties, but many times your problems might increase! Some people follow Jesus because it is the cool thing to do. But be warned, some of what Jesus says is frightening, and you might want to count the cost before you start following Him. Why? Because you will have to die! Here is an example from Jesus' own words: **"Then He said to them all, 'If anyone desires to come after me, let him deny himself, take up his cross daily, and follow me"** (Luke 9:23).

I have two questions for you. When Jesus was carrying the cross on his back, where was He headed? If you have a cross on your back, where are you headed? I will give you a hint. It is not an amusement park. It is a place called Golgotha, the place of the skull. It was where Jesus was crucified and died. It is also interesting that Jesus told those who wanted to follow Him, to do this daily!

We are told in the book of Romans 12:1-2 to offer our bodies as a living sacrifice while on this earth. If we are on the alter of sacrifice, a death will happen and this death is a real death, but not in terms of our physical bodies, but in terms of ungodly passions and desires. God has given us the gift of passion and desire, but the devil wants to pervert them. God wants us to keep our flesh in check, and not let the devil pervert our passions and desires. This is dying to our flesh.

When we deny ourself, we are dying to our fleshly lust, pride, and ungodly passions and desires. This is what I call *DTS*. DTS are three letters that stand for *"Dying to*

Self". Our sinful nature wants to satisfy the lust of the eyes, the lust of the flesh, and the pride of life. Our flesh is crying out for fulfillment. According to Paul, the flesh is at war with our spirit. But when we deny ourselves, we are figuratively killing the flesh and letting the Holy Spirit work in our lives.

In Galatians 2:20, Paul said, **"I have been crucified with Christ, and therefore I no longer live, but Christ lives in me. The life I now live in the body, I live by faith in the Son of God, who loved me and gave Himself for me."** As you get to know Jesus, you will have to crucify your lustful desires and follow the Lord every day! It is not something you did last month, or last week, it is a conscious thing you do every day! This is how you can show God that you love Him.

The reason that Moses and the others saw God was because they had died to themselves while they were alive. They were "walking dead men". They died to the lust of the eyes, the lust of the flesh, and the pride of life everyday. Shadrach, Meshach, and Abednego obeyed God at all cost, even at the cost of their lives! Because they loved God so much, they had made dying to their flesh a way of life. When they were given the opportunity in real life to show their love through obedience, they were thrown into the fiery furnace and experienced a mighty miracle of God. They saw One like the Son of God in the furnace with them!

"Whoever does not love does not know God, because God is love" *(1 John 4:8).* The most powerful force in the universe is love! The single greatest thing you can do with your life, and for the lives of those around you is to get to know Jesus Christ! Why? Because when you do, you will learn about true love and will be able to love yourself, God, and others! In order to truly love, you must get to know God!

As parents of 12 children, Diane and I want our children to know and love us. Not because they are forced to love us, but because they truly want to love us. This is true for all parents. We want our children to love because it is their choice and not ours. I know that we get this feeling from God our Father because we are made in His image.

In my opinion, this is one of the main reasons that God has shielded our eyes from seeing Him. God doesn't force anyone to love Him. God's presence is so AWESOME, yet His character is so humble. If we were to see Him in all of His glory, we would immediately want to be with Him forever. God has shielded our eyes from seeing Him because he wants us to know Him and love Him not because we are forced to but because we want to. God wants us to seek Him and love Him with our eyes of faith!

So if knowing God shows us how to love others, how can we show God how we love Him? **"He who has my commandments and keeps them, it is he who loves Me. And he who loves Me will be loved by My Father, and I will love him and manifest Myself to him" (John 14:21).**

If you want to show God that you love Him just obey His commandments. If you do, God says He may manifest Himself to you. But be warned, if God does show Himself to you on this side of death, it will be a frightening experience. Moses obeyed God's commandments, and God appeared before him. Even though Moses was very close to God, this is what he said of the experience of being in the manifest presence of God: **"And so terrible was the sight, that Moses said, 'I exceedingly fear and quake!'" (Heb. 12:21)**

SO WHAT ARE GOD THE FATHER AND JESUS LIKE?

The New Testament shares a lot about Jesus and through the Gospels we can get to know what He is like. There are glimpses of what God the Father is like in the Old Testament. But God the Father's character is clarified in the New Testament. When Jesus talked about the Father, the disciples were curious and wanted to meet Him. When Phillip asked Jesus to show the Father to them in John chapter 14, we are given a small window into what the Father is really like:

> **"Philip said, 'Lord, show us the Father and that will be enough for us.' Jesus answered: 'Don't you know me, Philip, even after I have been among you such a long time? Anyone who has seen me has seen the Father. How can you say, 'Show us the Father'? Don't you believe that I am in the Father, and that the Father is in me? The words I say to you I do not speak on my own authority. Rather, it is the Father, living in me, who is doing his work. Believe me when I say that I am in the Father and the Father is in me; or at least believe on the evidence of the works themselves'" (John 14:9-11).**

Jesus is the exact representation of the Father. The qualities of character, attitude, love, and sacrifice exhibited by Jesus are exactly what God the Father is like. They give up their life for us. This reminds me of a special person in my life. My wife, Diane. Thank you Sweety! You are a blessing! Our children wouldn't be the same without you, and neither would I. Love you!

Here Diane is doing her daily routine of homeschooling the kids.

"HE WHO FINDS A WIFE, FINDS A GOOD THING..." PROVERBS 18:22

The Elkton Record

Happy Mother's Day

May 14

A Publication of the RFD News

Ps 127:3-4 "Lo, children are an heritage of the LORD; and the fruit of the womb is his reward. As arrows are in the hand of a mighty man; so are children of the youth." (KJV)

A very special mom to her family, Diane Crevier is pictured with,(starting with front), Ben, 6; Hollie,7; Caleb, 16; Diane holding Nathan, 4 months; Bruce, holding Zack, 2; Micah, 4; Isaiah,15; Katie, 13. Not pictured, Jacob, 18.

Mom is special gift to family of ten

By Chris Schumcher
Elkton Record

On May 14 children will honor their mothers with flowers, gifts or possibly breakfast in bed. Special days such as this are set aside each year so recognition can be given to moms all over America who make countless sacrifices for the sake of their families and children.

Its typical to see families with one or two children loaded into a shopping cart, or being towed down an isle in the grocery store. It's also common to see a mom with a baby carrier hooked to the back of a bike with a toddler strapped in enjoying an afternoon ride, while mom enjoys some exercise.

But how would one manage this with ten kids? A challenge for any mom, but here's a story of one mom who manages to keep all the balls in the air, and maintain a close family relationship with lots of love sprinkled on top.

A short drive west of Elkton takes you to the Bruce and Diane Crevier home. The yard is filled with playground equipment and a monstrous RV sits idle in the driveway.

A young lady greets me at the door. I introduce myself and get ready to ask if her mother is home. The young lady, as it turns out, is the mother, Diane Crevier, who invites me in. Diane is holding four-month-old Nathan, whose bright smile and large eyes immediately melt my heart.

As husband Bruce joins us in the recreation room, which once served as a front porch, the quiet laughter of children can be heard from different parts of the house.

I begin our interview with the question, "What do you consider your biggest challenge raising ten kids?" With no hesitation, Diane responds, "Bruce and I want to make sure that our children have the best care and we train them up right - to have the best character."

The Creviers have chosen to home school their children, and both Diane and Bruce share in the educational responsibilities. "The older children have learned to manage their own time and know what is expected of them," Crevier said.

"The younger children observe what their older brothers and sisters are doing and follow by example."

The children spend the morning on lessons, or longer if necessary.

"We tell the children that the more diligent you are at your studies, the more free time you will have," the couple added.

Having a large family may not have been the plan from the beginning, but both Diane and Bruce are certainly no strangers to a full house. Bruce comes from a family of 12 siblings; Diane, a family of seven.

"Our parents were great role models for us to follow," said the couple. "First we thank God for His son Jesus and sending his son to save us. We would also like to thank our parents who gave us tremendous values to build our lives on."

Bruce spends about 200 days a year on the road supporting the Champions Forever ministry, and the family joins him about 75% of the time. The Crevier family, well known for their basketball skills and great entertainment their show provides, also needs a support crew. When the RV rolls, so does the whole family. Each of the children are responsible for different tasks. The kids are also a part of the team, and on occasion, so is their aunt Tanya.

"The kids continue their studies when we travel, and also have hobbies and interests they enjoy. They never seem to be bored."

The Champion Forever ministry takes the family all over

continued on back page

Code #3

CODE #3
CHAMPIONS MAKE JESUS CHRIST KNOWN TO THE WORLD

"Let your light so shine before men, that they may see your good works, and glorify your Father in heaven" (Matt. 5:16).

"And He said to them, 'Go into all the world and preach the gospel to every creature. He who believes and is baptized will be saved; but he who does not believe will be condemned'" (Mark 16:15).

"Now all things are of God, who has reconciled us to

Himself through Jesus Christ, <u>and has given us the ministry of reconciliation...</u>" (1 Cor. 5:12)

STORY #1: THE MYSTERIOUS ENCOUNTER

The man, who came out of the convenient store, was wearing black leather from his head to his toes and was headed in my direction. He was quite a large man, about 6' 4", and had tattoos on his arms. He had a black bandanna pulled tightly over his head with long light brown hair sticking out the bottom. His beard was long and he had it wrapped in a pony tail below his chin. As he walked toward me, I handed him a Gospel tract and he didn't look happy. His response was not what I was expecting! Lord, help me out?

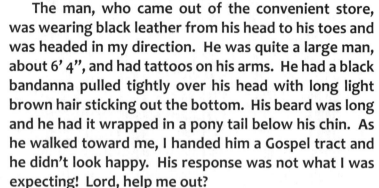

The above story took place at a gas station in Minnesota. Before my confrontation with this stranger, my family and I had been traveling for about five hours. It was 1:00 a.m. on a Friday night. As I was driving, my wife and I were visiting together while the kids were sleeping in the back of our 15 passenger van. We were on our way home from a basketball camp where we did a program for the University of Wisconsin, Green Bay earlier that day. We were more than halfway home. We were traveling west on Interstate 90, across the state of Minnesota. As I was driving, Diane and I glanced back to check on the kids in the van, and all the kids were sound asleep. All we saw were bodies laying everywhere with arms and legs hanging over seats and people. It had been a big day and everyone was exhausted. There was no movement and everyone looked awkwardly comfortable.

About a half hour later, I noticed that our gas tank was nearing empty. So to give our tank some needed attention, we pulled past Albert Lea, MN and stopped at a 24-hour gas station just off the interstate. As I pulled up to the pump, there were two other people filling up there as well. A pickup truck and a large Harley Davidson motorcycle chopper. The Harley was just on the other side of the pump from where I pulled up and the rider was not with the motorcycle.

SHARING CHRIST THROUGH A GOSPEL TRACT

When traveling, I have made it a habit to try to carry some Gospel tracts with me so that I can make the most of every opportunity. Gospel tracts are little booklets that share a story about the Gospel message of Jesus Christ. They talk about where we stand with God, what God has done for us, and how we can be born again into God's Kingdom. Because people had gone out of their way to share the message of Christ with me, I felt compelled to do the same for others.

When I stop at gas stations or other locations, I try to put some Gospel tracts out, or give them to people when I feel led to do so. Gas pumps are one of the places where I have put them. As I was filling up, I decided to put a tract on the pump. While I was pumping gas, I looked at the large Harley on the other side and because the driver wasn't with the bike, I assumed he was inside paying for his tank of gas.

I glanced again at the Harley, and I felt that maybe the Lord was speaking to my heart, "When the guy comes out of the store, you need to give him one of those Gospel tracts."

That seemed like a good idea, even though I didn't really feel like it. It was late and I wanted to get home, but I decided that when the owner of the motorcycle came out, I was going to step out of my comfort zone and hand him a tract.

YOU'VE GOT TO BE KIDDING

Suddenly, this big guy came walking out of the store and headed in the direction of the motorcycle. When I

saw him, I thought to myself, you've got to be kidding! Lord, I hope it is NOT that guy!

The man who came out of the convenient store was wearing black leather from his head to his toes and was headed in my direction. He was quite a large man, about 6' 4", and had tattoos on his arms. He had a black bandanna pulled tightly over his head with long light brown hair sticking out the bottom. His beard was long. As this big guy walked toward his bike, I tried to get his attention.

"Excuse me sir." I said, but there was no response.

"A Sir, excuse me, sorry to bother you," I said a second time as I made my way towards him and reached out my arm to hand him the Gospel tract.

"What? Huhhh? Yeah, what do you want?" He said in a grim voice as he looked in my direction as he was putting his beard into a pony tail.

"Ahhh, sorry to bother you, but I have a little booklet that I want to give you. It talks about how you can know the Lord and have your sins forgiven. God bless you," I said as he paused for a moment and took the booklet from me.

"What the %#&@ is this?" He said in that grim voice.

Most of the time when I hand out these Gospel tracts, people usually thank me for the gesture, but his response was not what I expected. So I turned away and started heading back to my van which was still being filled with gas. The man paused for a moment to look at the front of the tract, and then he responded. "Hey buddy, what is this? What did you give me?"

"Ahh, yeah, that booklet talks about how you can go to Heaven. Everyone will die someday, and we have sinned, but the good news is Jesus died for our sins." I said as I tried to explain what was in the tract.

"Does this thing talk about God? DOES THIS %@#& THING TALK ABOUT JESUS? Hey buddy, who do you think you are, giving me something like this?" He said with a loud-angry voice as he tossed the booklet on the ground.

He looked right at me, and his facial expression became scary! At this point, I really did not know what to say to this man, and the situation became very unpredictable. I could see that I had hit a nerve in him, and I certainly didn't want to start any trouble. I didn't say anything so as to not escalate the situation and start a fight with him. At this point, I just felt like jumping in the van and speeding away, but my van was still hooked to the pump, and I still had to pay for my gas!

He proceeded to walk over and sit down on his motorcycle. He pulled up the kickstand, leaned forward to look at me over the pump and continued to yell at me as he sat on his Harley.

"Hey you! Hey you! Who do you think you are giving me something like that?" He continued, "I want you to know that me and the man upstairs have an agreement. When I die, I'm gonna be JUST FINE! I will not need this #%@&! book from you, and I certainly don't need all this Jesus stuff. Who do you think you are giving me something like that? Huh? Are you some kind of 'Holy Roller' or something? Huh!?" He said in an expression that obviously meant that he was totally ticked off!

So I tried to diffuse the situation by answering him in the most calm and respectful way possible. "Sir, I didn't mean to offend you by giving you that booklet. The reason that I gave it to you, was because the information in that booklet changed my life, and I thought you could benefit as well."

Before I saw this man, I thought I had heard from the Lord. I thought God nudged my heart to give this man a Gospel tract. But from his response, that wasn't the case at all. I was totally mistaken, and now I was paying for my mistake! I hadn't heard from the Lord. I should have left well enough alone and minded my own business!

As I was thinking about what to say and do next,

75

something amazingly divine happened! This man was about to get a wake-up call, and it certainly was not coming from me!

In the next moment, all I heard was this **"CRASH!"** Then I heard this painful yell, **"OWWWW! AHHHHH! OWWWW!**

I looked over to where the biker was on the other side of the pump and to my astonishment, the guy's big motorcycle had fallen over and had pinned him on the ground against the gas pump! His big Harley was laying right on top of him! His right leg was caught under the right side of the large bike. His heavy bike was close enough to the pump that his head was bent to his chest and his body was being smashed between the bike and the pump! He was caught and could barely move. As I watched, he was frantically trying to push the bike up and off his body to shake himself loose, but the bike was so large and heavy that it was a feeble attempt. He went from this big burley guy to what looked like a trapped rat!

I quickly came around the pump and looked into his eyes. He looked up at me with his chin jammed against his chest. He could barely talk. He looked as shocked as I was!

It seemed like something you would see in a movie. I found myself a spectator for a few moments as he was below me frantically struggling to escape but to no avail. Then I came to my senses and quickly called to another man who was with his truck pumping gas opposite to where we were! He heard me and quickly ran over. Then we both proceeded to try to lift that huge Harley off this man. It was a heavy bike and we struggled, but we eventually got the bike up and off him and back on the kickstand. The big guy was now holding his right leg by the knee and from his expression, he was embarrassed and in pain.

"Wow, are you alright?" I said as he rubbed his knee.

"Ahhh owwww!" He moaned as he limped and struggled to get back to his bike.

"Are you alright!?" I said again.

"Yeah, yeah, I think I am going to be alright. It landed on my bum leg!" He said.

Just then the man paused and looked right at me. His whole countenance changed. His eyes went from being scary to being wide open. Like some incredible thought came to him. What he said next shocked me!

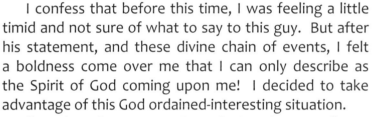

"Maybe the man upstairs is trying to tell me something!" He said.

I confess that before this time, I was feeling a little timid and not sure of what to say to this guy. But after his statement, and these divine chain of events, I felt a boldness come over me that I can only describe as the Spirit of God coming upon me! I decided to take advantage of this God ordained-interesting situation.

"You bet the MAN UPSTAIRS IS trying to tell you something!" I fired back as I thought to myself, *did I just say that?* Then I thought, I had better give him an earful while his leg was still hurting. With as much boldness as I could muster, I let him have it!

"Sir, the 'man upstairs' is trying to get your attention! I did not give you that little booklet to give you bad news but to give you good news. The bad news is you, like me, we are sinners. We have broken God's Commandments and are headed for hell, but the good news is Jesus died on a cross for your sins. He came to set you free!

"You see sir, God gave you a revelation of what is going to happened to you if you keep rejecting God. A minute ago, you didn't want anything to do with me, my booklet, God, or Jesus; that is until you found yourself trapped under your bike! There was no way out. You don't realize it, but right now you are trapped in your sins! You are headed for Hell, but Jesus Christ will help you escape Hell! That little booklet that you threw on the ground shows you how you can receive forgiveness

77

of sins and eternal life with God. But you rejected it because you have a hard heart! Someone died for you and you could care less! Sir if you died tonight, it would be too late. You need to repent before it is too late! To repent means to turn from your sins and turn back to God. Humble yourself right now, and let God give you a new heart!

"God listens to prayer, and Romans 10:9 says, **'If we confess with our mouth the Lord Jesus, and believe in our hearts that God raised Him from the dead, then you will be saved.'** You can receive God's gift, but you, sir, need a change of heart. If you want to pray right now and give God your heart, I will be glad to pray with you, but if not, I have to go."

This man looked at me with tears welling up in his eyes, he said, "Yes, I would like to pray with you!"

At that moment, we both bowed our heads and grabbed hands. Then as we started to pray, he started to cry. He asked Jesus to be his Lord, asked forgiveness for his sins, and humbly asked God for the gift of eternal Life in Heaven! I almost couldn't believe that I was praying with the same burley guy that just a moment ago was ready to beat me up!

After we finished, he gave me a hug and I noticed tears had dripped from his eyes onto his motorcycle gas tank. I then gave him the booklet that he threw on the ground and encouraged him to get a Bible, read it, and follow the Lord.

"Sir, my name is Bruce, what is your name?" I said as our eyes met again.

"They call me Chowder, and excuse me, Bruce, I want to thank you not only for helping get my motorcycle off me but for helping me get right with the 'man upstairs'"!

Chowder ended up leaving, and I could tell by the tears and by his attitude that he had a change of heart. It says in Scripture, **"Therefore, if anyone is in Christ, he is a new creation. The old has passed away; behold, the** new has come"(2 Cor. 5:17).

As Chowder drove off, I paid for my gas and we were soon back on the road. Diane was watching the whole thing from the van window, so she and I discussed what had just happened.

"Were you ready to come to my rescue if things got out of hand back there?" I asked as I drove down the road.

"Oh Yes, Honey!! I was getting ready to come out and rescue you from that Big Scary Guy!" She said as we both laughed!

With the confrontation with Chowder still vivid in my mind, I couldn't help but think, "Wow, did that just happen?" I came to realize that YES, it was the Lord that was prompting me to give that Gospel tract to him.

At first I thought he was a lost cause and that he wasn't ready to follow God, but I was mistaken. God's unseen hand turned a sour experience into a sweet time of repentance! What was so amazing was the fact that even though Chowder was a seasoned biker, God used the strength of his motorcycle to humble him and get to his heart!

God revealed to me that those people that you think are so far from finding the Lord are sometimes the ones who are the closest to finding Him and who need Him most. If you will be faithful in sharing Christ like what happened in this case, God will even provide a miracle to move a heart to make it happen! My attitude concerning sharing my faith with a hard hearted person changed that day.

By the way, I had so much adrenaline going after that meeting with Chowder that I drove the last three hours and wasn't even tired! We got home at 4:00 a.m.

79

STORY #2:
THE TRAGIC BLESSING

"I am so sorry, your friend, Bret, well, I hate to break the news to you, but he died last night." She said with sadness in her voice.

I was at college, and the cleaning lady broke the worst news ever. My best friend had died, and I was now confronting one of the saddest times in my life.

TWO YEARS EARLIER

(Knocking on my door)

"Come on in," I said as I was unpacking the rest of my stuff in my dorm room at school.

"Hey, my name is Bret, and I am the Resident Assistant on this floor."

"Nice to meet you, my name is Bruce, and I guess I am your next door neighbor." I said as Bret looked at my Bible verse that I posted on the outside of my door.

It was my first day at the University of South Dakota. I just moved into the third floor of Richardson Hall. I had just posted a large piece of construction paper with a Bible verse on the outside of my door. I wanted it to be a testimony to these guys in college about the love of God. The world was telling them a lie, and they needed to hear the truth. I wasn't going to let my fear of what people thought stop me from being a witness for Christ. If Christ had died for me then I was going to live for him. Before Bret came in my room, he saw the Bible verse.

"I noticed you had a Bible verse hanging on the outside of your door. Let's see here, it says, **'I am the way, the truth, and the life, no one comes to the Father, except through me" John 14:6.'** So why did you put this on your door? Are you a Christian or something?" Bret asked.

"Yeah, I am a Christian. Are you a Christian?"

80

"Sure, isn't everybody?" Bret said in a joking manner.

Transferring to the University of South Dakota during my sophomore year was a good move for me since I wanted to be closer to home. On my first day, I met this guy name Bret. He was the new Resident Assistant(RA) on my floor. As a matter of fact, our rooms were right next to each other. I was in room 329 and Bret was in room 330. As we talked and got to know each other, we found out we had a lot in common. We were both the same age, we both liked sports, we both played quarterback in high school, we both had the exact same motorcycle at college, we both liked to lift weights, we both liked cars, and I really liked his, because he had a beautiful blue Z-28. This guy could even spin a basketball on his finger. But the one thing that we didn't have in common was, I was a Christian and because he went to church every now and then, he thought he was a Christian. I could see by the fruit in his life that for Bret, being a Christian was just talk.

When we first met, Bret was a little apprehensive because he had never met anyone his age who was an outspoken Christian. But because we had so much in common, and because we were both athletes, he respected me. Honestly, for me it was like meeting a brother that I didn't know I had, and Bret felt the same way. Little did we know, but God had placed us as neighbors for a greater reason.

We started to hang out daily and had fun! After classes, we would take our motorcycles for a spin around Vermillion, South Dakota. Then, four times per week, we would find ourselves at the Dakota Dome lifting weights and workout together.

We became very close and also did some other crazy things, mostly late at night. To explain those other "crazy things" that we used to do, I need to give you a little history lesson:

THE WHISTLE FROM HEAVEN

When I was in the 8th grade I used to help out a local chicken farmer clean out his chicken coop. This coop was about a mile from our house, and was a really big coop with 10,000 chickens. Every 6 months the owner would hire some guys help him clean out the coop. After 6 months of feeding these chickens, the chicken poop was piled high beneath their cages. We are not talking just a little chicken poop. We are talking tons and tons of it! He had a special tractor loader that he would drive under the cages and would scoop up the poop from a pit under the cages. As he would take a big scoop, some of the poop would splash up onto the walkway that goes between the cages. It was my job to scoop that splashed poop back under the cages so he could scoop it on the next run. It was a dirty poopy job, but I got used to it.

Anyway, you never know what you are going to learn just doing the dirty work. While scooping poop, I learned one of the most valuable and useful skills in my life that had nothing to do with poop scooping. It is a skill that I developed and have used daily since I learned it during my scooping days. The skill, was learning how to whistle!

Now before this time, I could do just a regular whistle where I could whistle a tune. This new whistle was a whole new type of whistle. You see, I had a few friends who could whistle loud by putting their fingers in their mouth next to their tongue and then blowing really hard. They could whistle pretty good, but I wanted to learn a really loud whistle where I didn't need my fingers in my mouth. Because I worked on the farm, my hands would often get dirty and while cleaning out the coop the last thing I wanted in my mouth was poop contaminated fingers! I wanted a really loud whistle that I could do using just my mouth. During this particular time, I spent two days working eight hours per day scooping poop and I practiced whistling the whole time. I eventually learned how to whistle and over the years, that whistle has been perfected! I have been told by many people that my whistle is a whistle on another level. I can usually out-whistle the best of them, but I can't take credit for the whistle, for it was God who gave it to me! He knew I would need it during my life. I can only describe this whistle as a God ordained siren from my mouth.

After I met Bret, one day we were outside playing catch with the football, and I was trying to get his attention. So I cracked out my whistle siren and Bret's eyes got really big. When Bret heard my whistle for the first time, his reaction was priceless:

"WOW! Bruce. Where did you learn to whistle like that?"

"You will never guess where I learned to whistle like this. I learned this whistle scooping chicken poop on the farm! Would you like to learn?" I asked as I let another quick whistle fly.

"Yes I would. You are going to have to teach me how to whistle like that! That would come in handy! How do you do it?" Bret said as he tried whistling with feeble results.

"Because you are my neighbor, I suppose I will teach you, but it will take some practice. Good skills like this just don't happen, you have to work at them! If you are willing to pay the price and practice, you will get it," I said.

While we were in college staying up late, some of the other crazy things we would do late at night was this: We would do some push-ups then look in the mirror and compare our muscles. After we both came to the conclusion that my muscles were much bigger

and stronger than his, (Hey this is my book and I need to write the truth) we would put our faces really close to the mirror so he could see how I put my mouth when I would whistle. We would look in the mirror for a few minutes so he could watch my mouth position. Then he would try to mimic my mouth and practice the whistle.

"OK, Bret, you pull your bottom jaw out a little bit and stretch your lower lip so it is tight against your bottom teeth. Next, you curl your tongue against your top teeth and make a small opening about the size of a straw. This is so a small stream of air will flow through that small opening in your tongue and hit your tight lower lip. When you adjust everything correctly, you will begin to hear the air crackle. When that happens, keep practicing the mouth position that made the crackle. When you do, the whistle will be yours!" I said in an excited manner.

"Bruce, I have been practicing, but I don't know if I am going to get that whistle." Bret said in a frustrated tone.

"Well Bret, just get your mouth like mine and practice over and over. That's what I did. It took me a while as well, but you are a pretty talented guy. If you are determined, and if you keep practicing, by the grace of God you will get it."

Bret and I spent the rest of that first year becoming close friends. He claimed to be a Christian and was a nice guy, but he never read the Bible, and it was apparent that God wasn't the first thing in his life. We would have long discussions about Jesus, God, and what it meant to be a Christian. I would try to drop hints from the Bible about Christianity. Sometimes our discussions got a little heated as I would challenge him to take his spiritual life to the next level.

The end of our first year was upon us and Bret came to me with an idea, "Hey Bruce, next year, you should try to become a Resident Assistant like me."

"Hey, that sounds like a great idea!"

"They are looking for more RA's, so you need to talk to Mac, the dorm director, tomorrow. It would be something that will help you pay for your school as well."

"Yes, that would help out a lot. It would be great to have a job to help pay for school," I said.

So with his advice, I talked to the dorm director, and the next year, I applied to become a Resident assistant, and got the job. I was on the first floor and as it would happen, Bret's room was right above mine on the second floor. Because of the location of our rooms, we could open our windows, and he would stick his head out his window, and I would stick my head out my window. He would lay facing down and I would lay facing up. We would talk late into the night from our windows. We were about twelve feet from each other and would even play vertical catch with the football. He would throw the ball down to me and I would throw the ball back up to him. Every now and then, one of us would throw a bad pass. Since I was on the first floor, I would have to climb out my window and go fetch the ball. Sometimes to be funny, Bret would give me a bad pass just to see me have to climb out my window and get the ball! When we got tired of playing vertical catch, we would stay up late talking and playing catch with the football down the dorm hallway.

It was a good first semester, and now we were well into our second semester. God was slowly working on Bret's heart and I could feel an openness in his heart to the things of God.

"Hey Bret, Campus Crusade For Christ does a Christian outreach in Florida over spring break. It is called Operation Sonshine. They have Christian speakers and will give us an opportunity to be a witness for Jesus. Do you want to go? I think it would be fun and we could drive your Z-28 down to Florida."

"Yes, that sounds fun but I don't know about talking too much about Jesus. I mean it is OK to believe

in Jesus, but I don't talk to other people about Him. I just don't want to go overboard with it. For me, it would be great to hang out on the warm beach and to go some place warmer that South Dakota for a week. If I don't have to preach then it sounds fun."

"Hey, they are not going to force you to do anything you don't want to. But remember, Jesus did die for you.

"Yeah, yeah, yeah, I know. We will plan on it!" Bret said.

So we made plans and got all packed up. We left on a Friday after classes and headed to Florida for Operation Sonshine during Spring Break.

We drove pretty much the whole way through, but Bret got more sleep than I did. Every time I was driving, he was sleeping, but every time he was driving, I couldn't sleep because he was practicing his whistle. He kept practicing it over and over, and just three hours into the 24 hr. trip, he learned how to whistle!

"Fooooh, fooooh, Wheeeew, Wheeeew, Wheeeew, Wheeeew! Hey Bruce, I got it!" He said with the excitement of a little kid with a new toy!

"Yes, Bret, you don't have to tell me you got it. I am sitting two feet from you and I can hear you very well!" I said as he continued to whistle and drive at the same time.

He was so excited to have learned this new skill that he practiced the rest of the drive down there, all during our stay there, and also on the way back. It reminded me of myself. When I first learned this siren whistle, I was using it all the time as well. I must've been a good teacher, because by the end of that drive down there, his whistle was getting loud and my ears were hurting!

At the Operation Sonshine Conference, we heard some great speakers that really challenged us in our faith. Through a series of circumstances, God used others and me to bring Bret to the point where he committed his life to Christ. Now Bret was not only a friend but also a brother in Christ!

"You know, Bruce, when I saw that Bible verse on the outside of your door, I thought to myself, what kind of idiot would put something like that on their room door in a public University. I thought you were really crazy because at first you seemed like a Jesus freak. But now I can see why you did what you did. You were trying to be a witness for Christ. I had never met anybody before who was a bold committed Christian. Thanks for making a stand for Christ, for you have set a good example for me! Compared to what Jesus did for us, anything we can do for Him is worth it!" Bret said as we were getting ready for final exams in the spring.

"You are right, Bret. Jesus is worth it! Some people get embarrassed about Jesus but when Jesus was hanging on the cross, he wasn't embarrassed about us! The main reason that I put the verse John 14:6 on my door is because many people believe that all roads lead to heaven, but that is not what Jesus said. He said that He is the only way. I also put it on there because Jesus is the answer to all of life's problems. So many college kids are searching for answers in life. John 14:6 gives a lot of answers. If you are searching for a way in life, Jesus says He is the Way. If you are searching for the truth in this world of lies, Jesus said He is the truth. If you are searching to have a meaningful life, Jesus said He is the Life!!" I said to Bret as we ended one of our many discussions about Christianity.

At first, it was me teaching Bret but Bret was a

really smart guy. As he grew in his faith, he started to challenge and teach me things as well. We were sharpening each other in our walk with the Lord.

THE DAY THAT TWO LIVES WERE CHANGED

It was May, and Bret and I were getting ready for finals.

"Hey Bret, I have to go over and study for my accounting test, but I will see you later for our workout," I said.

"Sounds good, Bruce. I am going to drive my motorcycle over to a friends house and study for a test myself, so I will see you at about eight or so, and we will walk over to workout," Bret said.

"Sounds great! Hey, you better be ready for a tough workout, my friend!" I said as we gave each other a high five.

I headed over to the business school library and was going to study for about an hour. From the library, I could see the street in front of our dorm. After about 15 minutes, I saw Bret zip by on his motorcycle on his way to study for his test. I remember thinking, man, that looks fun, maybe I should skip this studying and jump on my motorcycle and go find Bret. Then we could go for a ride together!" I felt so blessed to have a friend like Bret, who was not only like a real brother, but also had become a brother in Christ.

About a half hour later I headed back to the dorm to get changed and get my stuff ready for our workout. My nightly plans were about to change for the worse as I was interrupted by another friend.

"Bruce! Did you hear the news?" John, a friend

said.

"No, what's up?"

"Bret got into a motorcycle accident just a few blocks from here!"

"WHAT? WHAT DID YOU SAY?"

"BRET WAS IN AN ACCIDENT!" John said.

"ARE YOU KIDDING? WHERE DID IT HAPPEN?" I said, not believing what I was hearing.

"It happened a few minutes ago just down the street," John said.

I couldn't believe what I was hearing. I had just been talking to Bret few hours ago, and then I saw him zip by on his motorcycle. We were going to workout tonight. This can't be happening.

I quickly dropped my books at the front desk. John and I sprinted the two blocks down the street. It was one of those times where I didn't want to get to my destination for fear of what I was going to see. As we approached the scene, I started feeling sick to my stomach. It seemed like it took forever to run two blocks. As we rounded the corner, we saw a bunch of police cars with flashing lights and police officers! When we came onto the scene, I saw three police officers and others moving Bret's smashed up motorcycle from the scene. Next to a tree, I saw splattered blood all over the ground.

"WHAT HAPPENED? WHERE'S BRET?" I asked a police officer.

"Looks like a car turned right in front of him. The ambulance just left for the hospital a few minutes ago. The young man was in pretty bad shape." The police officer said.

It was about a half mile to the hospital, so John and I sprinted to the hospital to see what had happened. When we got there, we had run so hard that we were out of breath. The doctors and nurses were in the emergency room trying to stabilize Bret's condition. We

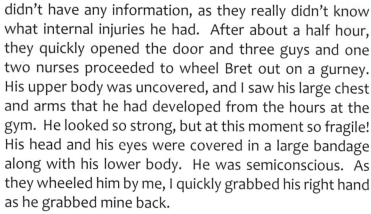

didn't have any information, as they really didn't know what internal injuries he had. After about a half hour, they quickly opened the door and three guys and one two nurses proceeded to wheel Bret out on a gurney. His upper body was uncovered, and I saw his large chest and arms that he had developed from the hours at the gym. He looked so strong, but at this moment so fragile! His head and his eyes were covered in a large bandage along with his lower body. He was semiconscious. As they wheeled him by me, I quickly grabbed his right hand as he grabbed mine back.

"Bret! Bret! Are you there, Buddy?" I asked.

"Yes." He said in a struggled voice, as we quickly made a connection.

Because of the bandage over his face and eyes, he couldn't see me, but he did recognized my voice.

"Bret, this is Bruce. I will be praying for you, buddy! God will help you. God will give you strength and you will pull through this. I will be praying for you!" I said as I felt a tears run down my cheeks.

Because of the injuries sustained in the accident, they transfered Bret to a larger hospital in Sioux Falls, SD. As the day progressed, nobody at school seemed to know any information. I tried calling his parents in Woonsocket, SD, but there was no answer.

In my room, I was in shock and still couldn't believe what had happened. I barely slept that night. The next day, I heard a knock on my door. It was Becky, the cleaning lady for our dorm hall. "Bruce, did you hear the news about your friend, Bret?"

"Yes, I did, Becky, he got into a motorcycle accident yesterday afternoon!" I said.

"No, the other news," Becky explained.

"What other news?"

"I am so sorry, your friend, Bret, well, I hate to break the news to you, but he died last night." She said with sadness in her voice.

"Oh, really? Seriously? Oh wow. Where did you hear that information?" I asked as I felt my heart drop.

"It was on the radio this morning. I knew you would want to know because I used to see you two together all the time," She said.

"Thanks for telling me," I said as I quietly shut my door.

With the door shut, I just stood there facing my door for about five minutes. I couldn't even move. I felt numb, and didn't feel like doing anything. Nothing mattered to me at that moment. I still couldn't believe what was happening. It was hard to believe that Bret was in an accident, but now this new information that he was dead, was too much, almost more than I could handle.

As I turned around in my room, I felt like a knife had gone through my heart. Even though I had known Bret for only two years, our hearts were knit together like brothers. It was like losing a flesh and blood brother that I had known my whole life. I thought about the workouts, playing catch, the talks, laughing, teaching him how to whistle, then having to endure his whistle, staying up late, him teaching me about cars, and me teaching him about Jesus, then him teaching me about Jesus. Lord, this can't be happening!

After I heard the news about Bret's death, I went and told John and then went home. I told my parents the news and they felt so sorry for me. I spent the next two days enduring one of the saddest times of my life.

Back at school, two days later, John came running over. "Bruce, I got some good news! Bret isn't dead! That was a false report on the radio!" John said with a smile.

"Seriously? That is the best news ever!" I said with expectation in my heart.

Bret hadn't died, but because of the seriousness of his injuries, the radio reported that he died. A

radio station had broadcast a false report based on his critical condition and that is where the cleaning lady heard the report.

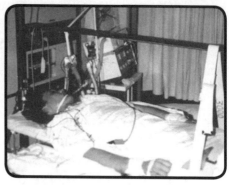

Bret had broken his pelvis and also his back. He was paralyzed from his waist down. He also lost his leg below the knee, and had to get fitted with a prosthesis. He went through 20 surgeries to get through his injuries, and spent the next year and a half going through rehabilitation. Then the doctors gave him more bad news. He was told that he would never walk again. Because he was an athlete, I could only imagine the devastation this was to my friend.

Later on, I was able to visit him while he was in Minneapolis going through rehabilitation. After the long time in Minneapolis, Bret lived at home for a while, so I visited him there.

"Bruce, I need something to strengthen my legs. I only have about 10% strength in them. Do you have any ideas?" Bret said on one of my visits to his home in Woonsocket, SD.

"Well, my dad taught me how to weld, and I have made some weight benches before. I think that if you had a leg press that was easy to use, and a weight bench, that would help you out."

So over the next couple of weeks, I built Bret, a leg press, a bench press, and also a speed bag punching bag rack.

"Bret, what do you think?" I said as we were setting up the equipment in his parents house.

"Bruce, this looks like it will work great. I can hardly wait to try it out."

By God's grace Bret beat the odds. With determination, hard work, and the prayers from family and friends, he has been walking with just a cane ever since. After he got out of the hospital and got back on his feet, he attended Law School. Today, Bret and his wife Marie have five children. Today, Bret works as an attorney in Sioux Falls, SD, and has written a book entitled, Tragic Blessing. You can order copies of his book at tragicblessing.com.

As Bret will tell you, even though he has had to endure a lot, it was because of the suffering of his accident that his walk with the Lord is deeper today than if he never had to go through what he did. God had brought us together for a reason. We both needed a friend. Bret needed a friend to show him the truth of his condition, that he needed Jesus, and I needed a friend who would sharpen me in my faith.

APPLICATION:
GO INTO ALL THE WORLD

After you God writes your name in his book, and you are filled with God's Spirit, you will have a desire to get to know Him. As you get to know Him, you will find that Jesus wants you to bear fruit. What is the fruit you are to bear? According to John 15, as we abide in the vine, which is Jesus, His vision will become our vision. His vision is that He is not willing that any should perish, but that all come to Him.

As you get to know Jesus, His burden for others will become your burden. When this realization came to the disciples, they caught the vision and it changed their lives. When this realization came to me and my family, we caught the vision and it changed our lives.

SHARING MY FAITH IS NOT MY GIFT

There are many who say, "Let those that have the gift of sharing their faith do it because sharing my faith is not my gift!" You are absolutely right! Sharing your faith is not your gift. As a matter of fact, sharing your faith is not any body's gift! Do you know why? Because sharing your faith is not one of the gifts listed in the Bible. Sharing your faith is not classified as a GIFT because sharing your faith is a COMMAND! God did not say, "Go into all the world and preach the Gospel, to you who are gifted." No, He said, "Go into all the world and preach the Gospel!" He calls everyone to the mission field. If you are alive, you are called!

MISSIONARY OR MISSION FIELD?

Why should we make Jesus known to our world? **If you are breathing, then you are either a missionary or you are the mission field.** All around there are people who need to hear the message, and you may be the only person who can reach them.

"But you just don't understand!" You say. "If I share Christ with people, they may reject me, or make fun of me, or call me names, or beat me up!" Yeah, you are right. They might reject you, and you may get embarrassed because of Jesus. But at the same time, those same people may also do what my biker friend Chowder did and what my best friend Bret did. They both heard the message and got their heart right with God! Just think, if you shared with someone, and they did commit to Christ, they will be forever grateful to you for stepping out of your comfort zone!

When you get to the end of your life, it will not be

the things you did that you will be unhappy about, but the things you didn't do that you will regret! If you have never shared your faith, you will regret it! When Jesus was hanging on the cross he was suffering and becoming a spectacle for you. Don't be afraid to be a spectacle for Him.

Did you know that Paul the apostle became one of the greatest missionaries of all time! He wrote half of the New Testament and ended up dying for his faith. Paul had the same fears that you and I experience when it comes to sharing our faith! He actually talked about sharing his faith, and gave us **The Five Qualifications for Sharing our Faith**. Here they are:

FIVE QUALIFICATIONS FOR SHARING YOUR FAITH

You may feel unqualified to share the message of Jesus Christ, so before you share your faith, make sure these requirements are met in your life. Maybe you have a few of these qualities as well.

Paul lists them for us: **"And I, brethren, when I came to you, did not come with excellence of speech or of wisdom declaring to you the testimony of God. For I determined to know nothing among you except Jesus Christ and Him crucified. I was with you in weakness, in fear, and in much trembling"** (1 Cor. 2:1-3).

1) Paul said he "did not come with excellence of speech". **Qualification number one: You are not supposed to be able to speak very well**.
2) Paul says, "For I determined to know nothing, among you except Jesus Christ and Him crucified." **Qualification number two: Ignorance or stupidity.**
3) **Qualification number three: "Weakness".**
4) **Qualification number four: "Fear".**
5) **Qualification number five: "Much Trembling".**

When you approach someone to share your

faith, if you exhibit any or all of these symptoms, **CONGRATULATIONS! YOU QUALIFY TO SHARE THE GOSPEL OF JESUS CHRIST!**

If you want to be a Champion, make sure you don't come to Heaven alone. If you make it to heaven and you come alone, that means that the ticket that God gave you, you jammed it in your pocket and never told anyone about it. Don't feel that you have to be a super spiritual to do it, you have all you need. True Champions, even in the face of rejection, make Jesus Christ known to a lost and dying world.

THE QUALITY IS IN THE SEED

In Isaiah 55:11, it says that God's Word is so powerful, that when it is shared, it will move hearts. If a farmer had some seeds in his pocket, then went out to a field, carefully planted those seeds, watered them and nurtured them, what's going to happen? They are going to grow, right? Now if a city-slicker were given those same seeds and went out and just threw them in the field. What's going to happen? Some of those seeds are going to grow as well. Why? **BECAUSE THE QUALITY IS IN THE SEED AND NOT THE SOWER!**

We are the sower and God's word, the Bible, is the seed. So many people think that because they don't know much or are not talented or are fearful, that they couldn't be effective for God. That is just what the devil wants you to think! It is not talent or skill that will save anyone. It is God and the power of His Word, the Bible, that will do the saving. Scripture says that it is through the foolishness of preaching that people get saved. According to Isaiah 55:11, when we share God's Word, God says that it shall not come back void, but will accomplish what God wants it to accomplish! So remember: **THE QUALITY IS IN THE SEED AND NOT THE SOWER!** Is is not easy, but I am here to tell you that it will be worth it all!

THE MINISTRY OF RECONCILIATION

When you follow Jesus, the natural progression is this: You repent of your sins, and He makes sure your name is in the Book of Life. Then you will have a desire to get to know the Lord, and you will catch His vision and His heart. What is His vision and heart. It is found in Luke 19:10. It says, **"The Son of man came to seek and save the lost."** The next thing you know, you too will be seeking and saving the lost. You will be in the ministry. If you can physically go into all the world, then go! If you can't go, then use your money to send someone! If you don't have any money, then pray for those who are need Him and those who are in the world witnessing.

The ministry that you are in, according to Second Corinthians 5:18-19, is called the "ministry of reconciliation". God, through Jesus Christ, is reconciling our hearts back to Him. Where does this Ministry of Reconciliation start? Acts 1:8 says, **"But you shall receive power when the Holy Spirit has come upon you; and you shall be witnesses to Me in Jerusalem, and in all Judea and Samaria, and to the end of the earth"** (Acts 1:8). Jesus gives us three locations that we will be ministering. Number one, Jerusalem; Number two, Judea and Samaria; Number three, to the ends of the earth.

1) MINISTER IN JERUSALEM

For the disciples, Jerusalem was close to home and was a good place to start. You might think that it is talking about being a witness to people close to home and it could be, but I believe that it was even more than that. Jerusalem was where the Temple of God was located and was where God dwelt. In the Old Testament before David would go into battle, he would inquire of the Lord. He would seek the Lord before making a move. (See 1 Sam. 11:3, 1 Sam. 23:2, and 1 Sam. 30:8). Before the priests would minister to the people, they too would come before the Lord and would minister to Him. Their example would be good advice for us as well.

Before we minister to others, we should minister to the Lord. Does the Lord need ministering to? Even though the Lord enjoys our fellowship, this ministry isn't for the Lord, it is actually for us. As we worship, fellowship, and pray to Him, the Lord will give us the grace and love that we need to minister to others.

2) MINISTER IN JUDEA AND SAMARIA

After we minister in Jerusalem, we minister in the outer areas around Jerusalem. These areas are called Judea and Samaria and figuratively represent our family and our friends. We are instructed to care for and rule our own houses because God is all about the family. It is so important that our families follow the Lord. If you feel you are called to go into all the world, and your family is falling apart, you need to get your family in order first, before trying to win the world to God. **"For if a man does not know how to rule his own house, how will he take care of the church of God?"** (1 Tim 3:5)

Next will be our friends. Scripture says that a prophet is not accepted in his own town. Sometimes family and friends can be the hardest people to win to Christ. Even Jesus had a tough time when He went to His home town. If Jesus is the Son of God, and had a tough time witnessing to those who lived by him, you will have a tough time as well.

To witness to family and friends, we need to remember the words of Francis of Assisi, who said, "At all times share the Gospel, and if necessary, use words." Don't be afraid to share about Christ, but with family and friends, your life testimony will sound just as loud as the words you speak.

3) MINISTER TO THE ENDS OF THE EARTH

Scripture tells us, **"And he said to him, 'Well done, good servant; because you were faithful in a very little, have authority over ten cities'"** (Luke 19:17). As you are faithful in ministering to and honoring the Lord, and as you are faithful to minister to your family and friends, God will open up the door so that you can minister to the ends of the earth. You can literally pass out tickets to heaven! To help you, we have a Ticket Illustration.

TICKET ILLUSTRATION for sharing your faith. It is a great story illustration on the choice that is before each person. I call this illustration, *A miracle with a piece of paper*. If you take a sheet of paper, fold it four times, and rip it once, you have the whole story of salvation in the English Language.

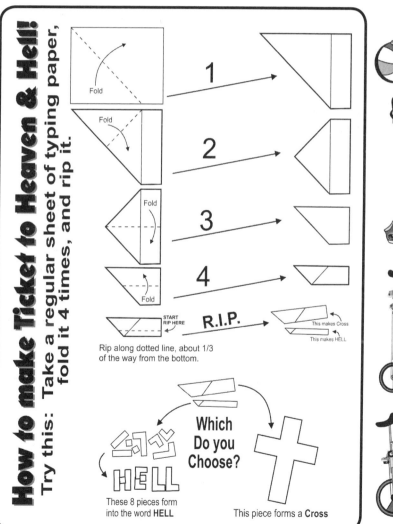

TICKET TO HEAVEN - The Story:

A Christian man named John, had a dream that he died and was standing in a line with hundreds of other people who had also died. As he looked around at all the people in this line, he only recognized one man, Bob, whom he had worked with while he was alive on earth.

When John's senses came to him, he realized that he was in line getting ready to stand before God in judgment! At this thought, John became fearful because he knew that he was about to stand before his Creator! Then John realized that during his life on earth, he had repented of his sins, and placed his faith in Jesus Christ and had been born again. Upon that thought, he noticed that he had a piece of paper in his hand. He looked down at the front of the paper which said, "John's Ticket to Heaven".

When he saw this, tears of joy and expectation came to his eyes. He was comforted and began to eagerly await the opportunity to meet God the Father, and His Son, Jesus Christ, who had died a horrible death on the cross for him.

John waved and made a motion to the man that he knew on earth. Bob came running over, after they greeting each other, John noticed that Bob didn't have a ticket to heaven in his hand.

"Bob, where's your ticket to heaven?" John asked.

"Ticket to heaven? What are you talking about?" Bob asked as he looked at the ticket in John's hand and then looked at his empty hand.

While on the earth, John had shared his Christian faith with Bob, but Bob rejected John and Jesus.

Bob didn't show any interest, and would sometimes make fun of John in front of the other workers. John didn't mind, though, and he would often pray for Bob. When Bob saw and read the ticket in John's hand, Bob became scared because he realized he didn't have one!

"John, where did you buy that ticket to Heaven?" Bob asked with a very concerned look on his face.

"Bob, you can't buy a ticket to heaven, it was a gift that you were supposed to receive while you were alive on earth. Remember? I told you that the wages of sin is death, but the gift of God is eternal life through Jesus Christ!" John said.

"Yeah, I remember you telling me about that, and I hated you for sharing that with me. I didn't believe you then but I believe you now! In school, I learned about evolution, where there isn't a God, and that we all came from monkeys! Oh I feel so bad now, I believed that there isn't such a thing as heaven, the devil, or sin! BUT I CAN SEE NOW. I WAS SO WRONG," Bob said.

"Bob, you believed the lie of the devil. He comes to kill, steal and destroy! He hates you and has lied to you, AND YOU BELIEVED HIS LIE! Here is the truth. When you accept Christ on earth, turn from your sins, and humbly receive Him, you become adopted into the family of God. This ticket you see in my hand, I didn't buy this. Jesus bought it for me!"

"Oh, John, I am so scared!! What should I do, John, WHAT SHOULD I DO?" Bob screamed as he noticed that it was getting closer to his turn to stand before God!

"Bob, I believe it is too late for you. According to the Bible if you do not believe in Jesus, before you die, God will not be your savior. He will be forced to be your judge. You will stand in judgment before God."

"John, can you give me some of your ticket?" Bob pleaded!

"No, Bob, this ticket has my name on it, and I don't think it is allowed."

"Come on! John! Please help me out! Please, Please! I believe in Jesus now! Help me! PLEASE HELP ME!" Bob exclaimed!

John, having a compassionate heart and being 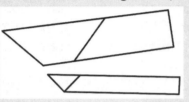 the generous man that he was, ripped off the bottom of his ticket and gave all of the pieces to Bob.

It was now Bob's turn in line. He was summoned by the angels to stand before God. As Bob approached the throne. The angels asked: "Where is your ticket?"

"Right here!" Bob shouted, as he handed his pieces of the ticket to the angel.

The angel opened up the ticket and all the pieces fell to the floor. Bob looked on, and was sweating  with anticipation! The angel picked up the pieces and assembled them together. They read the following:

God looked at the pieces and said, "Bob, I  brought people to you to show you the way but you rejected it. You lived for yourself and for your father, the devil.

"You mocked Me and My Son! It is too late. Depart to the place your ticket says, that place was prepared for you and your father, the devil!"

Bob screamed in terror as the angels hauled him away into everlasting death.

Then John approached the throne. The angel asked him for his ticket. The angel saw that it was like the one before and wasn't a whole ticket. John tried to explain to the angel that he was trying to help out Bob, and when the angel opened the ticket, it was this:

God then said to John, "John, Thank you for honoring my Son, Jesus! Thank you for not living for yourself, but for living for others and living to honor Me! Enter into thy JOY, thou good and faithful servant!

John Wesley was a great evangelist and was noted for appointing itinerant, unordained evangelists to travel and preach as he did and to care for these groups of people. Wikipedia.org

Here Josiah and Hollie are in England with a statue of John Wesley. He had his finger up so they taught him how to spin a basketball on his finger!

Bruce & Diane at five years old. The growing Family!

YEAR-END DOUBLE ISSUE
Sports Illustrated

The Beat
By Lisa Altobelli

IS SHE or isn't she? At **Andy Roddick**'s annual charity event last week at the Polo Club in Boca Raton, Fla., **Anna Kournikova** reportedly told fans she is now Mrs. **Enrique Iglesias**, claiming to have wed longtime boyfriend *(below)* in a secret ceremony in Puerto Vallarta, Mexico, earlier this month. "Enrique is great. Everything is awesome," she said. But on Monday there were reports that the couple was not hitched, and Kournikova's representatives had not confirmed the nuptials. Kournikova, 23, was married to NHL star **Sergei Fedorov**, who is dating ubiquitous party girl **Tara Reid**, proof that there is life after Anna.

PICTURE THIS Everyone's busy during the holiday season, but no one has more balls in the air than world-champion basketball spinner Bruce Crevier. The four-time *Guinness* record holder—he's spun 21 basketballs at a time—and South Dakota native performs around the country with his wife, Diane, and their nine children. Last week they spun through Omaha, entertaining fans at men's and women's games at Creighton University.

Code #4

CODE #4
CHAMPIONS BUILD THEIR LIVES ON THE ROCK OF GOD'S WORD

"Therefore whoever hears these words and does them. I will liken him to a wise man who built his house upon a rock: and the rain descended, the floods came, and the winds blew, and beat upon that house; and it did not fall for it was founded on the rock" (Matt 7:24-25).

"I am much afraid that the schools will prove the very Gates of Hell unless they diligently labor in explaining the Holy Scriptures and engraving them in the hearts of youth. I advise no one to place his

child where the Scriptures do not reign paramount. Every institution in which men are not unceasingly occupied with the Word of God must be corrupt."

Martin Luther

STORY: FIRM FOUNDATION

"Diane, you are not going to believe what just happened! Our new barn! The one that we just built! IT IS GONE!" I said with shock!

I wish the above statement didn't actually happen, but this story takes place in the summer of 2012. Diane and I were discussing plans to build a small structure to help store our performing equipment.

After Diane and I were married, we felt led to travel and minister as family. We believed that if God created the family, He could provide what we needed to travel as a family. Ever since the Lord put it on our hearts to start Champions Forever Ministries, God has been faithful in providing everything we have needed to make it all work. We wanted the whole family part of this ministry of encouraging youth and adults to be "Champions" in the game of life. This didn't happened overnight, but in Second Thessalonians 5:24, it says, **"He who calls you is faithful, who also will do it."**

When we travel, it is usually in a large converted bus. Before we had the bus, we had cars, vans, and other motorhomes, but they just weren't holding up to our intense travel schedule. Before we got the bus, we prayed about building a large shed to park it in. The shed was a physical manifestation to God's answer to prayer. After the large shed was built, God provided a bus.

On the back of this large shed, we poured a pad of cement. While that cement was still wet, I scratched a verse of Scripture into the concrete. It says this: **"For we**

know that if our earthly house, this tent, is destroyed, we have a building from God, a house not made with hands, eternal in the heavens" (2 Cor. 5:1).

This was written to remind my family and me that even though this large shed was nice, it is temporary. Someday, it will be like everything else on the earth, it will eventually rust, rot, and be destroyed. But the good news is God has a building for us in heaven that is eternal that will never be destroyed! Little did I realize, that later on, that verse would remind me and bring more comfort to my life than when I first carved it into the cement.

In the large shed, parked next to the bus is our tractor. Anyone who has spent a winter in South Dakota (SD) knows that the weather can be very unpredictable. We use our tractor to mow our pasture and to move snow during the winter.

When we first moved to Elkton, SD, we mowed a huge yard with a push mower and moved snow off of a long driveway with a shovel and our sweat. It was a lot of work. After our first blizzard, we found that the shovel was a joke, but I wasn't laughing! As I tried to tackle the huge piles of snow, the snow drifts were laughing at me!

To replace the shovel, a few years later, I purchased a walk-behind snow blower. I thought this is just what I needed! That is until I came home one night from a program at 2:00 A.M. I was confronted with a six-foot drift on our 100-foot driveway! Once again, Mr. Drift laughed at me as I attempted to move it out of the way. While the family slept in the van at the end of the driveway, I commenced my work. It took me two hours just to get a two-foot wide path through the length of the driveway! I spent the next four hours with the snow blower, plowing a path, just to get our vehicle near the house!

We ended up selling the snow blower, and God helped us purchase a John Deere utility tractor with a loader. It is four-wheel drive, and works great for moving

the snow. Believe me it gets a lot of use!

The problem with South Dakota is this. It will snow six inches and when you move the snow, you think you are done, right? No, no, no! Not so fast, you aren't done, for you've just begun! You end up moving that same snow again and again and even again. Ask me why. Why? Because of the SD wind, that is why. Get this. It won't even be snowing out, but that's OK, the wind makes it look like there's a raging blizzard outside. The wind will be sure to whip the same snow around for a few days, just to keep you busy. You know the stuff you moved off of the driveway, don't worry, it will be back in front of your car later in the afternoon! This works well at keeping all the farmers busy during the wintertime! As you can see, we are thankful for a tractor!

GROWING MINISTRY NEEDS A STORAGE SHED

"Diane, we have problem. Our large shed where we park our bus and tractor doesn't have room for our program supplies. It would be great to build a smaller one for storage. It would help to keep us more organized." I explained.

I agree, Bruce. Instead of a shed, why don't you make a small barn with a gable roof so you can have an upstairs for extra storage."

"Hey, that's a great idea! We could make a nice second floor and that would double our space. I am so glad I married you. For you have such great ideas." I said as I gave Diane a hug.

It says in the Scripture, that he who finds a wife finds a good thing and obtains favor from the Lord. God had blessed me, not just with a wife, but a wife who had a head on her shoulders. She was smart as a whip and is a large reason why we have been so successful with the ministry!

We decided on a small barn to help store some of the things we use in our ministry. "With the current cost of materials, and doing all the labor ourselves, I am thinking it would be feasible. I would like it to be the size of a small garage, say 16-feet by 24-feet. We have a little money saved up, and Kevin, the guy at the lumber yard, is good about letting us pay our bills as we go so it should work. There, how does something like this look, Honey?" I said as I scribbled a few ideas on paper.

"That looks great!" Diane said.

So with the plans written down and the materials in place, we commenced building our new barn. My boys helped, along with my brother-in-law, Steve Nelson. We took it step-by-step and after a few plan modifications and a few months of labor, the barn was completed!

"Hey boys, can you pick up those tools and those pieces of tin." I asked the kids as we were cleaning up for the last time.

"Sure, dad," Came the reply from the older boys.

The new little barn turned out great! The walls were covered in tan steel and the sidewalls met a green gable roof that looked like a beautiful medium sized barn. The dimensions were approximately 16-feet wide, by 24-feet long. The barn turned out perfect, and was the right size for what we needed.

"Ben, go get mom, and tell her the new barn is done." I said.

"Dad, mom is already coming! She is bringing us dinner." Ben said.

"Great! Are you guys hungry?" I asked, knowing that my boys are ALWAYS hungry!

"YES, YES, yes, Yes, Yes, yes!" Came the reply from too many voices!

Building this barn was definitely a group effort - Caleb, Isaiah, Josiah, Ben - and I were doing most of the heavy work and the climbing. Micah, Zach, and Nathan were our runners bringing us stuff, picking up stuff, and running errands to get us tools, screws, wood and tin from the big shed. Even my oldest son, Jacob and his

wife, Alicia, who lives about 1 1/2 hours from home would come up on the weekends and help as well. Our twins, Tori and Tessa, the youngest of the bunch, were doing their best to help out by getting in the way, moving stuff that didn't need moving, trying to hand stuff that we didn't ask for, and at the same time asking a multitude of questions. "Why do you do this? What's that for? What are you doing? Can I help? Here's a hammer."

Even though Diane, Katie and Hollie, didn't do much in terms of the actual construction effort, they were just as important in building this barn as those of us who were cutting the wood and using the tools. They were on the support crew and kept all the workers happy by bringing us water, snacks, and whole meals. If we needed an extra hand, they were right there to pitch in. Plus, they would also help us clean up after a day of making messes!

"Thanks so much Diane for the refreshments and all the great meals, not to mention helping us clean up every day. I couldn't have done it without you and the girls!" I said as I bit into an egg and tortilla and admired our new barn.

"Oh, you are welcome, Bruce. And my, that barn really turned out beautiful! You guys did a great job, and I am glad it got done in the early summer!" Diane said as she took a few pictures of the new structure.

"Thanks so much for your help, Diane, I believe we will get a lot of use out it. I thank God that we were able to build it. I definitely couldn't have done it without the Lord's help." I said.

Over the next couple of weeks, we moved stuff

to the barn that was going to be stored there and got everything organized. Everything was looking great.

"Where did we put all this stuff before we had this barn?" I said to Diane as the little barn was filling up with stuff.

"I don't know, but it seems to be getting full. That basketball shipment from China didn't help matters. Those boxes take up a lot of room." Diane said as we were stacking 70 boxes of basketballs.

About a month later, our family was outside, near the new barn just visiting. As we were talking, we looked over to the western sky. We could see a thunderstorm brewing in the distance.

"Diane, have the kids put in their bikes, it looks like we are going to be getting some rain." I said as we finished our talking.

"Yes, I will tell them," Diane said.

As we watched the approaching storm, we noticed it looked like some of the clouds had a green haze to them.

"You know, Bruce, my mom used to tell me that when you see green clouds in a storm, it is not good. It means that there may be a lot of wind." Diane said as we were putting things away.

"Yes, those clouds do look kind of green. Even though it is very calm outside right now. I just wonder if this is the calm before the real storm." I said in agreement as the sun was starting to go under the clouds.

About a half hour later, we looked at the weather report, and it said that there was a thunderstorm and tornado warning with possible damaging winds. As we observed the approaching storm, it was getting darker and looked like early evening. The clouds in the west were now in front of the sun, and those same clouds looked very menacing.

"Hey Bruce, I am going to take the little kids in the house and go into the cellar," Diane said as she headed

113

into the house.

"That would be a good idea, Honey. The boys and I will move the cars to the opposite side of the house, pick up those last few things, and join you in the house." I said.

Diane headed into the house, while - Caleb, Josiah, Ben - and I made the last few preparations before the storm. Then it happened!

Diane's Green Sky Wind Prediction came to pass because one second, it was totally calm outside, and the next second, the most unexpected fierce wind that I have ever experienced in all my years in South Dakota came straight out of the west. The boys and I were about 50-yards from the house. The wind came up so fast that we couldn't even run to the house. Our large shed was nearer, so we made a mad dash!

"Boys, run to the shed!" I shouted as we sprinted to take cover.

We made it to the shed just in time. Once inside, we made sure all the doors were shut! While we were standing next to the bus, it suddenly became so loud inside the shed that we had to yell at each other just to communicate. The wind became frightening. There are not enough adjectives to describe that ferocious, devastatingly, awesome, crazy, loud wind from the storm! As we looked out the windows from the shed, we saw debris flying by the windows, branches, and different things from our yard. We would later find out those winds were over 120 miles per hour!

Our attention shifted from the windows, to the large roll up garage door on the west side of our shed. Our whole shed was creaking from the wind, and the roll-up door was bulging from the tremendous pressure of the wind. Then a second later, we watched as the whole door push inward into the shed just like some giant hand had shoved it right in! The power of the wind broke the garage door side rails and rollers like toothpicks. The large door was hanging by the top springs, flapping in the wind like a rag doll.

"BOYS, RUN FOR COVER IN THE BUS! THIS WHOLE SHED MIGHT BE DESTROYED! I said as we quickly made our way into the bus.

Once in the bus, the boys and I cried out to God in prayer for safety. We also prayed Diane and the rest of the kids were safe in the house.

We had heard of people describing tornado winds that sounded like a freight train, and they were right! We experienced the sheer sound of uninhibited wind power. When you hear a freight train driving by, wide open, horn blaring, and you are standing five-feet from it, that is what we were experiencing! But this out of control freight train was off the tracks, holding nothing back, and plowing right through our property!

As we peaked out the door of the bus, things weren't looking good, for I could see daylight light coming from where the top of the wall met the ceiling! I thought to myself, Is the shed roof gone?

The wind at this point started to subside and now all we could hear was heavy rain. We tried to look out but it was still rather dark just as the sun was starting to peak through the clouds in the west.

We ventured out of the bus and made our way to the door of the shed. As we opened the door, what met our eyes was shocking to say the least. Trees, branches, and devastation was everywhere. I quickly ran to the house to check on Diane and the rest of the kids. On the way, I noticed shingles from the house strewn all over the yard. I got to the door and I turned around. To my shock the roof from the large shed WAS GONE! I looked to the right, and our new barn WAS GONE! The wind had destroyed both of them.

Diane met me at the back door, she and the rest of the kids were just fine.

"Diane, you are not going to believe what just

happened! Look! Our new barn! The one that we just built? IT IS GONE! Look, the roof of our large shed. IT IS GONE!" I said with shock in my voice.

"Wow, OH MY, BRUCE, WOW! WHERE DID IT GO? I DON'T SEE IT ANYWHERE!" Diane said as we looked at the devastation.

"Look over there! It looks like one of the walls of the barn is in that tree. The rest of the barn must have been blown away!" I said as we walked closer to where the barn used to be.

As we surveyed the damage, everything was out of its place. Our property, and my brother, Marc, who lives 1/4 mile west of our house, had a direct hit from the wind. There were trees, branches, shingles, pieces of tin, our trampoline, and various debris scattered all over the yard. The equipment and basketballs that we put into our new barn were strewn all over the yard! We even had debris in our yard from my brother Marc's house.

After about 45 minutes of surveying the damage, we decided to drive into the town of Elkton, which is one mile east of our house. As we entered town, we saw most of our green shed roof had traveled one mile and pieces were all over in a grove of trees. We even saw a piece of our green tin roof, wrapped around the street sign as you enter town. The devastation in

the town was amazing. As we drove around, everyone in town was trying to pick up the trees, branches and debris.

After we came back home, we were picking up the pieces, and I walked by the cement pad that I had carved that Bible verse in. I reread the verse and it said this: **"For we know that if our earthly house, this tent, is destroyed, we have a building from God, a house not made with hands, eternal in the heavens"** (2 Cor. 5:1).

FRIENDS TO THE RESCUE

After I prayed, we were feeling a little overwhelmed by all the damage and about a half hour later, some neighbors who are our friends from a local Hutterite Colony drove by our house. The colony has nine brothers who live there, with their wives and children. They saw the damage, so they went back to their colony and came back with 10 of their young men armed with chain saws, a large tractor bucket lift, a truck and various other equipment. They helped my brother and I clean up the big stuff in our yards. A couple weeks later, some friends from Sioux Falls, Brian and Deb Taubert, and their family, came and helped us pick our roof out of a grove of trees a mile away. God answered our prayer and it brought tears to our eyes.

As we were cleaning up, I was still in shock that our brand new barn, the one we spent so much time, money, and effort on, was totally destroyed! A few pieces of the shed that were laying around the yard, were reminders of the freight train winds that plowed through our property.

We were thankful that more damage wasn't done. We were also thankful to God for Insurance, for we were able to re-roof our large shed, and we were able to rebuild our small barn.

We spent the rest of the summer cleaning rebuilding and picking up all the pieces. Here is a picture of the shed roof that we picked up that had traveled over a mile away.

I learned a valuable lesson that day, the hard way. To save money, I cut a few corners when we built the little barn. Plus, I didn't have a good foundation to strap it down like I should have. When we observed some of the scraps of shed around the yard, you could see some of the nails that had been pulled out by the strong winds.

To learn from my mistake, when we rebuilt the shed, I decided we were really going to beef it up! I put extra effort into it the second time around. Instead of nails, we used 3.5 inch screws on everything and extra screws on the parts that we felt may be weaker. We also put hurricane straps on all the walls and on all the rafters. For the foundation, we put four screw anchors in the dirt, at each corner of the shed. Each anchor will hold 10,000 pounds. To each anchor we hooked cables that are wrapped around the top of the walls. If another wind like that comes up, the barn today is better equipped to handle it.

APPLICATION: CHAMPIONS BUILD THEIR LIVES ON THE ROCK OF GOD'S WORD

God allowed our barn to be destroyed to remind me of the importance of a good foundation! You see, God gave me a second chance to prepare my barn with a better foundation and stronger materials. Maybe right now, you are going through a life storm! You are having a difficult time and your foundation is not built on the Rock of God's Word! We have great news! God is giving you a second chance to build your life on a firm foundation!

God wants us to have a firm foundation, so when the storms of life come our way, we will be able to withstand them. The word of God will not only give you strength through the storms of life, it will also give you wisdom in relating to God and to man. It will help you in every area of your life, and I don't know about you, but in my life, I can use all the help I can get. Scripture says, **"If any of you lacks wisdom, you should ask God, who gives generously to all without finding fault, and it will be given to you" (James 1:2).**

When my wife and I were first married, we prayed to the Lord, "Lord, we don't know how to raise a family, but you do. Lord we don't know how to do ministry, but you do. We pray that You give us wisdom in all areas of our lives, so we can be a testimony for You!" We fall short in many ways, but with the Lord's leading, He has been answering that prayer. We have a long way to go in our faith walk. We certainly don't have all the answers, but we know where to find them.

It also says in Psalms 119:105 **"Your word is a lamp unto my feet, and a lamp unto my path."** There are times in my life where I have felt like I am walking in the dark. When that wind storm came through and did all that damage, I had to ask, "God, what are you doing here?" When I quieted myself, I felt that small still voice speak to my heart, "Read my Word, and trust Me." I did go to the Scripture, and God gave me comfort. No matter what has happened in our lives as a family, God has been right there for us!

FOUND: GOD'S PHONE NUMBER

After you ask God for wisdom, God will direct you to a textbook where you can learn wisdom. That textbook is the Bible. **B – I – B – L – E** stands for **Basic Instructions Before Leaving Earth.** It is the owners manual for Life. If you buy a new lawnmower, new TV, or new computer

they usually come with an owners manual. It's a small booklet that tells you how to operate the device. Also, an owner's manual usually has a 24 hour toll-free number that you can call if anything goes wrong with your device.

The owners manual for life, the Bible, also has God's 24 hour toll-free phone number as well. If anything goes wrong in your life, you can call the number. Oh. What? You don't know God's phone number? It is a good thing you are reading this book, because we are going to give it to you! God's Phone number is --- 333! It is a toll-free number, you can call it anytime, day or night, and you don't even need a phone! It is Jeremiah 33:3, and that verse says, **"Call to me and I will answer you and tell you great and mighty things you do not know."** God is waiting to hear from you, so give Him a call today!

GETTING A GRIP ON GOD'S WORD

If you want to be a Champion with a strong foundation in life, you MUST build your life on God's Word! One of the best ways to have a firm foundation is to get a GRIP on God's word.

HEAR GOD'S WORD

This is represented by your hand and starts by hearing the word of God. "Hearing" is represented by your pinky finger. **"So**

then faith comes by hearing, and hearing by the word of God: (Rom. 10:17).

If you want to build your faith, you first must Hear God's word. Listening to God's word through a sermon or someone else will build your faith. But if that is all you do, it is like holding a Bible with just your pinky. If someone tries to pull the Bible from your hand, your grip is so weak that you would not be able to hold it. In the same way, when problems in life come your way, you will not remember God's promises. Your faith is weak.

READ GOD'S WORD

Let's say you get some initiative. You decide that in addition to hearing God's word, you are going to start reading God's word. Scripture says: **"Till I come, give attention to reading, to exhortation, to doctrine"** **(1 Tim. 4:13).**

The ring finger represents Reading God's Word. Along with hearing God's Word, when you read it, you are hearing from God yourself. When someone pulls on the Bible, your grip is stronger, but you are still weak in your faith.

STUDY GOD'S WORD

You decide in

addition to hearing and reading God's Word, you are going to Study God's Word. Scripture says in 2 Tim. 2:15: **"Study to show yourself approved unto God, a workman that needs not to be ashamed, rightly dividing the word of truth."** (The middle finger is one of the strongest fingers and represents Studying God's Word.) When you decide to Study God's Word, you will see Scripture take on a new dimension, and your understanding will increase. Your grip on God's word and your faith is slowly getting stronger.

MEMORIZE GOD'S WORD

Hearing it, reading it, and studying it are great, but if you want to strengthen your walk, then obedience will bring your faith to a new level. David tells us how to obey God in the book of Psalms: **"Thy word have I hid in mine heart, that I might not sin against thee" (Psalms 119:11).** Hiding God's promises in your heart means you Memorize God's word. This will help you to obey God, and when you obey God, it shows that you love God. (Read John 14:21) Memorizing is represented by the pointer finger. Your grip and your faith is getting strong. If someone tried to pull the Bible out from your hand it would be tough, but there is still room for improvement.

MEDITATE ON GOD'S WORD

Some people think that to be prosperous and successful you need a college education or a good job with benefits. That's not what God says. Joshua 1:8

says: **"This Book of the Law shall not depart from your mouth, but you shall meditate on it day and night, that you may observe to do according to all that is written in it. Then you will make your way prosperous, and then you will have good success."** If you want to be prosperous and successful, God tells us what we need to do. Meditate on His word day and night! To meditate is like a cow chewing its cud. After the cow eats the grass, he regurgitates the food and chews it up over and over. It helps digestion and is good for the cow. In the same way, when we continually think about God's word His thoughts become our thoughts, and His wisdom becomes our wisdom. Meditation is represented by the Thumb, and is the only finger that can touch each of the other fingers. When we hear it, read it, study it, and memorize it, then we can re-chew all of those actions by meditating on it day and night. It increases our faith. With the thumb helping to grip the Bible, your faith has become extremely strong!

APPLICATION IS THE KEY

Dear Reader, don't stop there! If you were a weight lifter who could bench press 400 pounds, and I told you a secret

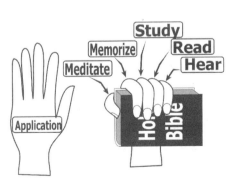

technique of how you could double your strength and bench press 800 pounds, would you be interested? Of course you would!

If you want to be a true faith powerhouse, there is a technique that you can do! You can actually double your faith strength. Scripture says: **"But be doers of the word, and not hearers only, deceiving yourselves." (James 1:22)** When you Apply what you have learned in God's Word, you can double the strength of your faith.

Application is represented by the other hand! Instead of holding the Bible with one hand, you are now holding it with two, doubling your grip! Your faith can now withstand the storms of this world and to top it off, when you apply what you have learned, YOU ARE GOING TO BE BLESSED IN WHAT YOU DO! Read it for yourself: **"But he who looks into the perfect law of liberty and continues in it, and is not a forgetful hearer but a doer of the work, this one will be blessed in what he does" (James 1:25).**

THE GRIP OF A CHAMPION

Before you die, become a Champion by building your life on the Rock of God's Word! Just look at that GRIP! That, my friend, is the GRIP of a Champion! It would be difficult to pull the Bible from those hands! That is the kind of faith you want in your life.

If you take a hold of God's Word, and you Hear it, Read it, Study it, Memorize it, Meditate on it, and then Apply it to your life, you will be a powerhouse in the faith! Get a GRIP on God's Word and Go For IT!

Code #5

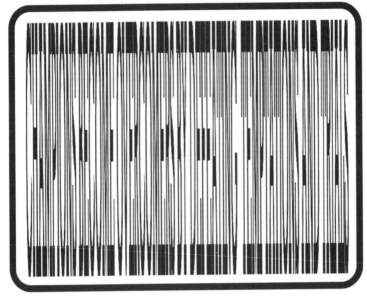

CODE #5
CHAMPIONS BECOME OVERCOMERS BY DEFEATING TEMPTATIONS AND TRIALS

"For whatever is born of God overcomes the world. And this is the victory that has overcome the world- our faith" (I John 5:4). "And they overcame him by the blood of the Lamb and by the word of their testimony, and they did not love their lives to the death" (Revelation 12:11).

WHAT DOES IT MEAN TO OVERCOME?

Overcome: To succeed in dealing with (a problem or difficulty): To defeat (an opponent); prevail

There was a time when Jesus was going through His suffering, that everyone left Him. He was rejected by all, even His closest of friends. Because of love for the world, even God, His Father, choose to turn His back on His only Son. During His most difficult struggle, Jesus was alone, sentenced to death, and was literally being buried by those who hated Him. **In the eyes of His enemies, Jesus was being buried! But in the eyes of God, Jesus was being planted!**

When the darkness comes upon you, and you are feeling lonely and rejected remember a seed. To be fruitful, it has to die. When the seed is in the ground, it is dark, cold and lonely. If you are struggling and feeling lonely, God has not forgotten you, so rejoice and don't lose heart! It is during these moments that God is planting you and using your struggle so that you can grow from a forgotten seed into an overcomer, just like Jesus!" God the Father is fighting for you. He wants you to become an OVERCOMER!

When I was a little boy, I was inspired by my older brothers and sisters to become a great athlete. I was literally living in the shadow of legends. I saw their trophies, and their accomplishments and I would try to practice, but it didn't quite work out like I anticipated. Every miracle starts with the platform of a problem. In the following true story, God used my problems, weaknesses, and struggles, to show me that He is greater than anything that comes my way! God showed me that with His strength, all things are possible.

STORY:
THE LITTLE PIECE OF PAPER

"Hey Bruufff! Hey Bruufff! Ha Ha Ha! Hey Bruufff! How you doing, Bruufff! Ha ha ha ha!" Two boys said to me as they past me in the hall way.

I wish they would stop making fun of the way I talked! I thought as I tried to ignore them.

My worst fear was coming true. It was my freshman year at Jefferson High School, in Jefferson, South Dakota, and I had a problem. When I was in grade school, nobody made a big deal about it, but I had a problem with the way I talked. I grew up with a speech impediment. Because I had grown up with all the kids in the Catholic grade school, they knew and accepted me and didn't make fun of me. But now that I was in high school, there were a lot of new kids, and some of these kids were cruel. It was to the point where a few guys were making fun of me on a daily basis. Going to school became a chore. Whenever I would see those guys, I tried to avoid them but they would make sure to find me and hurl their insults. I felt like hiding, and if I couldn't hide, I felt like getting in a fight with them just to make them stop. Since I had become a Christian the year before I knew that was not what God wanted. I tried my best to ignore them and do what the Bible instructed "turn the other cheek".

One night I was praying to the Lord: "Lord, what is going on? Why is my speaking so different? Please help me to say my words right." I prayed.

I had really never listened to the way I talked before, so I was curious as to what I sounded like. My older brother had a tape recorder. One night during my freshman year, I borrowed his tape recorder, went into my bedroom, shut the door, and started recording myself as I read a book. I reluctantly played back the recording and my fears were confirmed. I could understand myself just fine, but when I spoke certain words, they sounded

funny. So I recorded myself over and over, again and again, trying to correct my speaking by talking differently, but nothing was helping. From that moment on, at school I became very self conscious of how I sounded. As I would talk to people, I knew what I sounded like and it made me not want to talk to anyone.

I played quarterback, and I also punted and kicked, on the freshman football team. The quarterback position requires major communication skills. Before I got into high school, playing football was no big deal, but now that some of my peers were noticing that I talked differently, my confidence level took a nose dive. I was able to play, and people could still understand me OK, but I knew some of my words sounded funny.

During Christmas that year, I got encouragement by watching a kid's movie called *Rudolf the Red Nosed Reindeer*. There is a scene in the movie where all the other reindeer were noticing that Rudolf had a bright red nose. It was making all the other reindeer upset. So Rudolf's dad made Rudolf wear mud on his nose to hide the shiny nose from everyone. This mud made Rudolf look and talk funny. Because of his funny talking and his red nose, he was rejected by some of his reindeer friends. As I watched that kid's movie, I could relate to Rudolf and thought about my struggle.

If you have seen the movie, you find out that good ol' Rudolf saved the day and ended up taking his weakness and making it his strength. Rudolf saved Christmas. I was praying about what I had seen in the movie. Maybe God could do something with my life as well, but things just kept getting worse.

My mother worked for the high school, in the front office as the secretary. It was nice having her there, and she encouraged me to take a speech class. As my sophomore year came around, I enrolled in speech class thinking this might help my speaking.

On my first day of speech class, the teacher had

each student stand in front of the class, introduce ourself and for a few minutes talk about who we are. It was difficult. When I stood in front of the class and tried to articulate my thoughts, I kept thinking about my speech problem, and it left me embarrassed. I ended up quitting the class after that first day. In my mind I knew there was no way that I would ever take speech class again!

Being a Christian brought even more ridicule. Jesus had become my friend, so I would carry my Bible with my other books. I would try to find strength by reading my Bible in between classes and during study hall.

When some guys saw me carrying my Bible around with my school books, they started calling me "Father Bruce", as a mockery of me being some kind of priest. Every time they would say it in front of others, it was like a dagger in my heart. Sometimes they would make fun of the fact that I was a Christian with a speaking problem.

"Father Bruce, oh, I am sorry, I guess it is Father Bruufff, Ha ha ha ha!" They said, knowing that there was a Catholic Church in town with a priest.

"Bruce, why do you carry your Bible around all the time? I noticed that you don't drink and party with the other guys at school? What do you want to become a priest or something?" Mike, a classmate, asked me one day in study hall.

"No, I don't want to become a priest, I just like reading some of the Bible stories because it gives me encouragement. As far as drinking, I want to become the best athlete I can become, and for me, drinking is not part of the program." I explained.

"But those Bible stories are just a bunch of outdated boring stories! What's the use of reading them?"

"Well, some of the stories can be boring, but there are a lot of exciting things that I have learned that apply to today. Some of those Bible verses give me strength."

129

This was a dark time for me, but my friend Jesus and God's word, the Bible, brought me comfort. As I would read, I was trying to figure out what the Lord was doing in my life since this speech problem seemed like a trial with no end.

On top of this, all of my four older brothers were First Team All-State Football Players in High School, and they all played college football! They were such an inspiration to me. I too loved both football and basketball, but being the smallest of my brothers, I was literally living in the shadow of legends. On the football team I wasn't the biggest or the fastest player and the pressure to succeed in football was a constant reminder. I remember thinking that someday my mom and dad and my brothers would be proud of me because I will be a good football player like them.

The Crevier brothers were just a couple farmboys from Jefferson – tenacious on the gridiron but "gentlemen" off of it. To this day, those who coached the Creviers say they were ...

'THE TOUGHEST BOYS I'VE EVER BEEN AROUND'

"Bruce, you know the tradition of your older brothers. Maurice, Marc, Ray, and I were all First Team All-State football players. You gotta keep up the family tradition. Work hard and maybe you can be an All-Stater like the rest of us!" My older brother Bert said one day when he was home from college.

"Yeah, I know, Bert. I have been practicing both football and basketball. You guys have really inspired me! As a matter of fact, I bet I have practiced more than all of you. I am hoping to be just like you guys. I just wish I was bigger and faster!" I said.

During this time, I had read a verse in the book of James that was kind of confusing. It said, **"Consider it pure joy, my brothers and sisters, whenever you face trials of many kinds, because you know that the testing of your faith produces perseverance" (James 1:2-3).**

Being a new Christian, I knew some verses that gave me hope, but where was God when I needed Him? I was under the impression that God was going to help me with my struggles. Sometimes I would doubt my belief because it didn't seem like God was doing anything good in my life! How was I supposed to find joy in life, with people making fun of me? I didn't know what God was doing, but I wanted to believe, for it was all I had to hang onto.

"Jesus, I don't know what's going on here, but help me to trust you! Help me to consider this pure joy because I don't see any joy in my life. I need your strength and your joy in Jesus name, amen." I prayed.

The summer before my sophomore year, my sister, Tanya, had given me a book by a former all-pro football player, Bill Glass, entitled, _Expect to Win_. In the book, he said that if you have a goal, you need to write it down on a piece of paper, and put it somewhere where you can see it everyday. It sounded like a good idea to me, so I wrote down "All-State Football", and below that I wrote the Bible verse Philippians 4:13, which says, **'I can do all things through Jesus Christ who gives me strength".** I stuck it on my bookshelf in my room, and I would see that every morning when I would wake up for

that whole next year.

The beginning of my junior year came and I was looking forward to football season! Our last year's starting quarterback had graduated and I was next in line for the starting position.

"Bruce, are you ready for football season this year?" My brother Bert asked.

"Yeah Bert, I have been running, lifting weights, and practicing all summer. Last year's quarterback graduated, since I was second string last year, I should be first string this season. I am really looking forward to starting!" I said with anticipation as I pondered the upcoming season.

You are the last brother in our family! If you are going to make First Team All-State, you will have your work cut out for you! Your brothers and I will be cheering you on! We hope you do well this year!" Bert added.

"Thanks, Bert, for the encouragement. I will definitely try to do my best." I said.

On the first day of classes my junior year, my mother got me out of class.

"Bruce, there is a speech therapist visiting the school this morning. I want you to meet with her." Mom said as we walked to the front office.

"A speech therapist? Do you think she can help my talking?" I said with anticipation.

"I don't know, but it is worth a try." She said.

I had never met with any therapist before, and in the school office I met with this lady who had me read some words. After she analyzed my speaking, she gave me a few exercises to try while she coached me. After about 30 minutes of practice, the words that seemed so difficult to say, I was starting to pronounce with clarity.

"Bruce, I am impressed! You are one of the best students that I have ever had. You are catching on very quickly, but you still need a lot of work. Go home and continue to practice those exercises that I taught you so you don't fall back into your bad speaking habits." The therapist instructed.

Over the weeks that followed, I practiced over and over and over again the speaking exercises that the therapist gave me. I couldn't believe it! I was slowly making progress and eventually I was CURED!

My family encouraged me, and was starting to notice a difference. I thanked, and thanked God for hearing my prayer. I prayed, "Jesus, thank you for curing my speaking!"

My speaking was a victory, I was so happy! But on the first day of football practice, my plans for starting at quarterback were fading, because there was a change of plans. At that practice, I noticed that there was a new player on the team. His family had moved so he transferred in from Sioux City West, a large school, to play on our team. It just so happened that this guy was a senior, he played quarterback, and if that wasn't bad enough, he also punted and he kicked. All the positions I was planning on playing!

I wonder if he is any good, I thought as we were warming up.

After the first practice, my curiosity was answered! His name was Tom. He was fast, he could throw, he could kick, and he ended up beating me out of all three positions: quarterback, punter, and kicker. The coaches barely gave me a glance. I was devastated! Tom also turned out to be a nice guy, so I was happy for him, but inside my dream of following my brothers' success was all but gone. In my mind, I heard my brother Bert's comments, "Bruce, you have to keep up the family tradition by making All-State Football!"

This unexpected turn of events was very disappointing as a player. My junior year turned out to be the longest and most frustrating football experience of my life!

Honestly, there were days that I felt like not going

133

to practice and just quitting the team. I felt the Lord asking me a question: "Bruce, are you still going to work hard and support the guy who beat you out?"

Reluctantly, I said, "Yes, Lord, I will try to work hard, and yes, I will do all that I can to make Tom a success."

I had made it a point to change my attitude. During practice, I would play catch with and encourage Tom. I tried to not let the lack of playing time change my attitude. During my junior year, I mostly sat the bench, but I did get to see one offensive play as quarterback. Tom had gotten shaken up during a play, so I went in to take over while he recuperated for that one play. As I ran onto the field, I thought, now is my chance! On that play, I dropped back for a quick pass, and I got blindsided and sacked! For me, this was a not a football season to remember.

After that season, I can remember my brother Bert didn't talk much about the All-State football thing, because I knew he was feeling sorry for me. Even though he didn't say a word about becoming like them, he didn't have to say anything, for it was ringing in my mind's ear.

The season ended and I felt like a whipped dog. I went home after the last game and I looked on my shelf, there was that crazy little piece of paper with my goal, "All-State Football" and my Bible verse, "Phil. 4:13". There it was, but now it was covered in dust and hidden in the back of the shelf by some books. I had purposely put those books there because I didn't like looking at it. But it was still there, reminding me and now condemning me!

I felt like that stupid little piece of paper was screaming at me. "Bruce, you are not good enough!" I picked it up, and was going to tear it up and throw it away, but for some reason, I didn't. I did put those books back in front of it. When I put it back, I looked at it between the books and just stared at it for a minute, and I thought, how can a little dusty piece of paper be so little, but yet so powerful at the same time? Bruce, what were you thinking? Writing some thing like that down? You didn't work hard enough, and even if you did, you don't have the tools it takes to be what you want! Sure God loves you and everything, but God doesn't let you just be what you want! You need to just accept the fact that God's plan for you does not include being an athlete on the level of your dreams! Let that stupid little piece of paper be a reminder, don't set goals like that, because you are going to get BURNT!"

My hope of following in the family tradition of All-State Football, was now out of the picture. How can a guy go from not playing at all in his junior year, to All-State football. Tom, the quarterback who beat me out last year, was better and faster than me, and he didn't make All-State. In my mind, I had to come to grips with the fact that I was going to have to settle with being the brother that didn't quite measure up!

SENIOR FOOTBALL SEASON

The summer before my senior year, like all the summers before, I lifted weights, I ran, and practiced, but because of my disappointing experience, I mostly practiced and did my workouts for something to do and out of habit. As fall rolled around, I was a little apprehensive about the football season, but at least I felt in shape.

Our fall two-a-day football practices started, and beings most of my classmates had played as starters the year before. They all knew their positions. At the first practice after we all did our

conditioning drills, the coach was lining up everyone in their positions. I thought for sure that I would be a shoe in, and the coach would have put me in the quarterback position but surprise, surprise! The coach was sure of every position on the field except for three positions. It was the quarterback, punter, and kicker positions.

They were the positions that I thought would be a no-brainer for the coaches, because I was second string last year. But beings I didn't play much the year before, it was like the coach forgot who I was. Wow, I was shocked. The coaches had tryouts for the quarterback, punter and kicker positions. As things go, I was going to have to win back all three positions. God gave me favor because it went well. The hours of practice paid off, and I was going to be starting quarterback punter and kicker.

THE LITTLE RULE

After our first week of practice, Head Coach Greg Young and Coach Larry Becker and I were in the coaches office discussing some plays. Out of the blue, Coach Young shared something from the <u>High School Football Rule Book</u>.

"Hey Bruce," Coach Young said, "I was reading the football rule book the other day and I found an interesting rule. Did you know that there is a rule that says that if the opposing team is punting the football to your team, you can do something called a "free kick"? If your punt receiver can fair catch the football, your team can do a "free kick" on the first play of that possession. From where they mark the ball, instead of your team lining up in a regular offensive formation, your team can line up in a kickoff formation."

"Why would you want to line up like that?"

"Get this," he added. "From there, your kicker can kick the ball off a tee, just like a kick-off. You basically kick the football back to the opposing team. Your team will lose possession of the ball, but listen to this, if the kicker can kick the ball far enough to make it through the goalpost, your team will get three points! Your team would basically be kicking an uncontested field goal off a tee! The other team can't block it, because it is a kickoff."

"Wow, Coach Young! That is an interesting rule." I said in amazement as I filed that rule in the back of my mind. Little did I know that information was a miracle puzzle piece from God!

WAGNER - THE NUMBER ONE RANKED TEAM

We started the season and the Jefferson Blackhawks were playing pretty well. Our record was 3 wins and 2 losses. We were well into our season and had four games left. It was our sixth game, and we were playing the number one ranked team in our state, Wagner, SD! Wagner was a great team, and they were undefeated!

It was the fourth quarter, and our team was doing great considering this was the first ranked team in the state. The score was 8 to 6 with Wagner in the lead. We were coming down to the final three minutes in the 4th quarter and Wagner had possession of the ball on their own 10 yard line. It had been a tough game, even though we weren't in the lead, the coaches were pleased that at least we were staying with them.

Announcer: "Alright Blackhawk fans, the score is Wagner – 8, Jefferson – 6. Let's hear it for our Jefferson Blackhawks!" (Applause)

THE LITTLE RULE REVISITED

"Come on Blackhawks! Let's see that defense! Coach Young yelled to the team.

"Do you think we can hold 'em coach?" Asked Jeff Rabbit, the keeper of the stats.

"I hope so. Wagner is on their own 10 yard line, and it is third down with eight yards to go." Coach Young added.

Wagner tried a pass play, but it was incomplete!

"Good Job Defense! It is fourth down and eight! It looks like they are going to have to punt from their own end zone!" Coach Young shouted from the sidelines.

The Wagner team lined up in punt formation, as Jefferson got ready to receive the punt. Trent Irwin was our punt receiver. From where Wagner was punting, we would have decent field position.

As our punt receive team ran onto the field, my thoughts came to me, and the Lord quickened my mind. I remembered the "free kick" rule that Coach Young had told me about before the season!

I quickly ran over to him and shouted, "Coach Young! Remember the rule you told me about? We are only two points down! Tell Trent to fair catch that ball and we can try that 'free kick' rule, where we line up in kickoff formation!"

"What? Bruce, what did you say?" Coach Young said as he was trying to remember.

"You know, the free kick rule that we talked about in the coaches office! Have Trent fair catch that Ball!" I said with desperation.

Coach Young remembered the rule and his eyes got really wide. He just lit up! He ran toward Trent and started shouting with his hands close to his mouth:

"Trent! Trent! Fair catch that ball! Fair catch that ball, Trent! FAIR CATCH THE BALL!"

Trent waved back to confirm that he heard Coach

Young.

Wagner punted the ball, and the punt was high. Trent waved his hand in the air to signal the fair catch and caught the ball on Wagner's 35 yard line. It is first and ten for Jefferson.

Coach Young grabbed my jersey with one hand, and by my face-mask with the other. He pulled my face as close as he could to his face and had the most serious look on his face that I had ever seen!

"OK, BRUCE, THIS IS IT! You know what to do, line up the team in a kick-off formation, and kick us a field goal. From where you line up, you will be kicking a 45 yarder (35 + 10) I believe YOU CAN DO IT! Get us "3" points buddy!" Coach Young said as he patted me on the helmet.

IS THIS REALLY HAPPENING?

The team huddled up, and I told them the plan. We lined up in kick-off formation. When the opposing coach from Wagner saw what we were doing, he made a big fuss and said, "Hey what's going on here? They can't do that! Hey, REF! What are they doing? They can't do that! It's an illegal formation! STOP the play! What is going on here!"

"It's in the rule book coach, settle down! It is called a free kick!" Said the head referee.

Lord, is this really happening? I thought as I ran onto the field.

I remember getting the kickoff team lined up, and as I was setting up the ball on the tee. Under my breath I was praying up a storm, and God quickened my mind to a verse in 1 Sam. 2:30, **"...those who honor me, I will honor."**

Was God orchestrating this time for me to kick a field goal. I couldn't believe what was happening. I remembered all those times of kicking the ball, practicing, running, doing push-ups etc. They were coming to head in this one moment. All I could do was say a short prayer to the One Who's unseen hand seemed to be guiding this whole event.

As everyone was lined up, and while I was adjusting the ball, I quickly said a final prayer. "Father in Heaven, in Jesus Name, I thank you for this opportunity to try to kick this field goal. You are the one who planned this, but Lord, I need your help! Please give me the strength to do it, Amen." I said as I put the ball on the kicking tee.

With the kicking team all lined up, I paced back a few steps and waited for the referee's whistle. I looked at the goal post in the distance and wow, it seemed like such a long way. There was a slight breeze in my face, and I wanted to wait until it subsided, but it was no use. Our huddle time for this play was about up, and we could not wait any longer.

I ran toward the ball as I had done thousands of times before with as much force and concentration that I could muster, I kicked that ball as hard as I could! SMACK! Before I knew it, the kick was up and away. It quickly sailed toward the goalpost! When my foot hit the ball, the kick felt good. It looked like it was on target, but was it long enough. It felt like slow motion, but it was going, going, GOING, AND YES, IT WAS LONG ENOUGH. IT WENT STRAIGHT THROUGH THE UPRIGHTS! IT WAS A 45-YARD FIELD GOAL!

My brother Bert, who had come home from college to see my game, was standing under the goal posts. I saw him jumping up and down!

The crowd from Jefferson erupted in a roar! All the Jefferson players ran onto the field, jumping up and down, and then headed right toward me! BOOM! I then received one of the worst tackles of my life, by my own team! I was on the bottom of the pile, and I could barely breath, but was enjoying every minute!

The game was not over. There were almost 2 minutes left in the game and we were certainly not out of danger. Because of the field goal, we kicked the ball off to them again. With the remaining time, our defense was able to stop them. They ran out of time, and we won! We beat number one ranked Wagner, SD with a final score of 9 to 8!

Wagner went on undefeated the rest of the season, and won the state football title in South Dakota. Their only loss that season, the Jefferson Black Hawks.

WAS GOD REMEMBERING?

Our season ended, and our team had some great moments! We didn't make it to the playoffs, but that didn't matter for we had beat Wagner!

A week after Wagner won the State Championship, Coach Young called me into his office. "Bruce, you did a great job this year, and you have some pretty good stats. I believe your 45 yard field goal against Wagner was a state record for longest field goal in South Dakota High Schools! I want you to know that even though we didn't make it to the playoffs, I am going to put your name up for First Team All-State. It will be a long shot, but you never know." He explained.

"What? Wow! I don't know what to say coach! I mean, thank you so much." I responded.

So I left his office, and couldn't believe what the coach said. I thought, Lord, what are you doing?

Could it be? That little piece of paper in my room, the one that had dust on it, that condemning little thing that I felt like throwing away. The little piece of paper that I wanted to forget about. Was God actually remembering it?

A couple weeks went by, and one Saturday morning, my mom woke me up at 7 am.

"Bruce, the phone is for you, it is your brother Bert!" She said.

I ran and picked up the phone, "This is Bruce," I said as I heard Bert shouting on the other end of line.

141

"Bruce, Bruce, did you see the newspaper, did you see it? You made it buddy! You made it! You made First Team All-State, eleven man team in South Dakota!" Bert shouted with enthusiasm.

"What? Seriously? Are you kidding me?"

"Bruce, You made it! You did it! You made my day, and God let you keep up the family tradition! Great Job Little Brother! I am so proud of you!" Bert said.

"Wow, Bert! Thanks so much for the news! I can't believe it!"

After I got off the phone with Bert, I had to run to my bedroom because I couldn't contain the tears. Halfway down the hall, the tears were flowing. When I entered my room, I got on my knees, and prayed. "Jesus, you did it. There is no way that I could have done it, but You did it for me. I couldn't speak but You healed me. I didn't have confidence, but You gave me confidence. I wasn't a very good football player, but You gave me strength to overcome. I wasn't good enough to make All State, but you gave me favor. Lord, I don't know what to say. Thank You so much!"

The next day at school, I ran up to Coach Young and gave him a big hug, "Coach, thank you for believing that I could do it!"

"That's OK Bruce, you did a great job this year, and you deserved it."

A true miracle had happened in my life. There is no way that I could have overcome if God would not have put the puzzle pieces in place and orchestrated things the way He did.

God taught me a valuable lesson that day. When you think that God has forgotten, or is too busy for the least of the least, you are wrong. You might be in a cold and lonely place in your life. But God hasn't forgotten about you! He is separating you and putting you in that lonely place so you will rely only on Him. He does this because He loves you, and because He is planting you to

Blackhawks Squeak Past Wagner, 9-8

by Kelly Kruithoff

A 33 yard touchdown pass and a first down field goal helped the Jefferson Blackhawks defeat Wagner, 9-8, in football action Friday, September 10.

The Blackhawks took the lead with 8:13 left in the first period as quarterback Bruce Crevier completed a 33 yard pass to Trent Irwin. The Point after was blocked and Jefferson led, 6-0.

Wagner took the lead 1:28 before the half as quarterback Curt Gau completed a 37-yard pass to Don Koeer for a touchdown. Wagner's two-point conversion try was successful and the team led 8-6 at halftime.

Jefferson's winning score came in the fourth quarter after a Wagner punt deep in the Raider's territory. The Blackhawks made a fair catch near the Wagner 30 yard line and elected to attempt a field goal instead of taking a first and ten. The gamble paid off as Bruce Crevier made a 45-yard field goal.

According to Blackhawk Head Coach Greg Young, the free kick field goal has been in the rule books for a number of years and can be done anytime after a punt anywhere on the field. Young said he tried the play "because Bruce Crevier is a good kicker". Wagner did not rush the kick and was deployed to catch the ball in case it fell short.

Wagner threatened late in the fourth quarter but was stopped by the Blackhawks on a fourth and one on the Jefferson 14.

Jefferson had a total of 148 yards in the game, with 75 yards gained on the ground and 73 yards in the air. Wagner totaled 181 yards, with 106 passing and 75 rushing.

For the Blackhawks, Trent Irwin led the team with 58 yards, gained on three passes. Tim Trudeau added 25 yards on the ground. For Wagner, Chad Soulek collected 32 yards. On defense, Chuck Corder had eleven tackles for the Blackhawks.

Young said the Blackhawks played much better the second week and a number of holes in the line were filled, giving the team more depth. He added the defense played tough, especially in the fourth quarter.

On Friday, September 17, the Blackhawks will host Akron Westfield Westerners. Game time is 7:30 p.m.

Five Crevier brothers made all-state teams

BY TERRY HERSOM
thersom@siouxcityjournal.com

Bert Crevier has no difficulty remembering the dates when his mother and father passed away.

Everything else about the 40-year marriage of Ray Crevier and the former Patricia Ricker was more than a little magical.

There simply had to be a little more poetry to the way it all came to an end.

"They died on each other's birthdays," said Bert, one of six sons and six daughters in a family that thrived on the deep religious faith and almost unparalleled work ethic instilled by two exceptional parents. "It was almost like they were a gift to each other."

Ray Crevier, a fighter pilot in World War II, didn't make it back to Jefferson, S.D., until July of 1947, nearly two years after the war.

A few days later, he met Patricia, a Briar Cliff College junior from Marcus, Iowa, and took her for a plane ride.

Two weeks after that, they were married.

"He knew right away that she was the one," said Bert, a test pilot in Baltimore, Md., and one of four brothers who followed in dad's footsteps, learning how to fly.

Marty Crevier, the eldest child, was already an athletic 6-1, 200-pound youngster when he died tragically at the age of 12.

Bruce Crevier

Ray Crevier Jr.

Bert Crevier

Somehow, it was as if his 11 younger siblings, some of them not yet born, made sure to treasure their lives in his honor.

Prime case in point: The five sons who reached adulthood all became South Dakota all-state high school football players, emulating another of their father's passions.

Maurice and Marc, the two eldest after Marty, will be inducted this weekend into the Ashland (Ohio) University Hall of Fame, honoring their football careers for a tradition-rich NCAA Division II program.

Graduates of Jefferson High School in 1968 and 1969, respectively, both were four-time all-staters for the Blackhawks' eight-man program, which enjoyed a 39-game winning streak spanning all but its first game under Matt Mottice, the coach for five seasons.

Younger brothers Ray Jr. (Class of 1972), Bert (1978) and Bruce (1983) also garnered all-state laurels and continued on to college football – Ray Jr., a defensive back, at Navy; Bert, a linebacker, at Dakota State; and Bruce, a punter and quarterback, at Bethel in St. Paul, Minn.

Bruce, though, has become more famous for the many world records he's established running basketballs and traveling the globe with his wife, Diane, and their 12 children, performing a memorable act that has them on the road upwards of 250 days a year.

And, he was simply following in the footsteps of an older sister, Tanya, who was first to build a barnstorming act around spinning and dribbling basketballs by the dozens.

"That was our claim to fame, Maurice and I, we brought that home from Ashland," said Marc Crevier, one of seven Creviers, Bruce and Tanya included, who make their home in Elkton, S.D., 20 miles south of Brookings.

Bill Musselman, the young Ashland basketball coach when Maurice and Marc were enjoying their All-America football careers at the school, spiced up a few of his halftime shows with basketball showman "Crazy George Schauer." And, before long, two-sport standout Jay Hoover had picked up enough to teach his roommate, Maurice Crevier, how to spin a basketball.

"Marc came the next year and we wound up teaching Tanya how to do that," said Maurice.

Show business aside, Ashland's Crevier brothers, Maurice at linebacker and Marc in the offensive line, inspired their younger brothers to fulfill the family tradition as football all-staters.

According to a 1994 story in the Sioux Falls Argus-Leader, Bruce felt the burden of his older brothers' success, pushing himself to maintain the tradition.

"I read a book by Bill Glass entitled, 'Expect To Win,'" said Bruce. "It said if you have a goal, write it down and stick it on a mirror so every morning it's staring you in the face. In the seventh grade, I put up a note that read 'all-state football.'"

And, the youngest brother's drive to excel was only just getting started when his all-state football accolades kept the family's football legacy perfect.

For a family with so many collective accomplishments, maybe the parents could only appreciate it all from a celestial vantage point.

Patricia Crevier was only 63 when she died of cancer on April 28, 1988, her husband's 66th birthday.

Ray was 72 when cancer also ended his life, passing away on Dec. 19, 1994, the day the love of his life would have turned 68.

grow to be an overcomer.

When you love God, He is orchestrating everything, both the good and bad things in your life to give you victory, and all for His purpose and glory! **"And we know that all things work together for good to those who love God, to those who are the called according to His purpose" (Romans 8:28).**

Making First Team All-State against such great odds opened my eyes to so many things! One thing was the fact that life is not about talent, and it is not about knowing who you are in the eyes of the world. It is about getting to know the loving heart of God and learning who you are in the eyes of God! Once you know who you are in the eyes of God then you can start walking in the victory that God has given us through Jesus Christ!

FINDING DESTINY THROUGH FAMILY & AIA

My first semester, I went to college at Bethel College in Minneapolis, MN, but eventually transferred to the University of South Dakota (USD Coyotes) where my sister, Ann, was attending. I loved my family, and this was closer to home. Plus, I also wanted to try out as a walk on player for the USD college basketball team. I shared my desire to play college basketball with some people, and they just laughed at me. "You won't even make the team, you are too short!" They said.

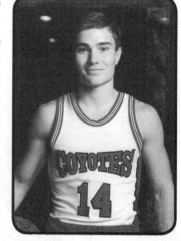

Maybe they are right, I thought. So I started believing them and then decided not even to try out. One day at school, I read the verse in Matthew 19:26 which says, **"With God, all things are possible."** This reminded me of what had happened my senior year in high school as God gave me victory against the odds. To prove myself wrong and to overcome my fear of failing, I set a goal to try out. With God's help, I made the team by the skin of my teeth! It was intimidating, for I was the last and the smallest player on the team. I sat the bench for my whole first year, but I didn't care! God came through once again. I had made the team, and I was excited.

Playing basketball in college was like having a full time job, and because I wasn't getting any game playing time, I decided to put my efforts toward becoming a better student and basketball handler so I quit the team my second year. This gave me time to study and practice my basketball handling and spinning skills.

During my college years, I had a desire to follow in the footsteps of my older sister, Tanya. Tanya is ten-years older than me. She was inspired to do basketball tricks by a guy that went to college with our older brothers. His name was "Crazy" George Shauer. They called him "Crazy" because he could do some crazy things with the basketball! He had a basketball handling show and Tanya was inspired! He taught her some tricks, and she practiced. She got so good that she was turning heads in the basketball world! In College, Tanya started performing at camps, schools and basketball halftime shows. I was her little shadow growing up, and would practice right alongside of her. She taught me how to spin the basketball, and also showed me some dribbling tricks.

During my growing up years, Tanya would take me with her on different performances. She would use her show to try to encourage the kids to make the right choices. When I saw the impact that she was making in the lives of others, it inspired me to do something positive with my life as well. As I got older, I continued to practice and perform with Tanya. Then God opened the door, and I started performing my own Spin - tacular Basketball Show around the local area. Here's an article

that was done when I was a sophomore in college.

During my junior year in college, a friend told me about a basketball team called Athletes in Action (AIA), that traveled around the USA and to other countries. It was a Christian Ministry Basketball Team that used the sport of basketball as a platform to reach  others with the gospel message. People who might not go to church might go to a basketball game and at the game the coaches and players would share their faith in Jesus Christ.

After my initial contact with them, they seemed like pretty cool people and I decided to go for it. Over the next two years, I raised some money, and ended up going on two summer basketball tours with two different teams. I went to South America one year, and the next year went to Spain and Russia. On these trips, my eyes were opened and God gave me a burden for the lost! It was during these tours that I came to the realization that God was calling me to do something for Him with my life. God's love had impacted me profoundly and I had seen it impact others as well. *I came to the conclusion, that if Jesus had died for me, the least that I could do, was to live for Him.* But, I had one problem: I had to overcome my fears of not being good enough, or tall enough for the game of basketball, or smart enough to know how it was all going to take place in my life.

It was during this time that my best friend, Bret

Merkle was going through rehabilitation. When I went back to college after my second summer tour with AIA, I crossed paths with and met a new best friend! This new best friend was a girl, her name was Diane, and she was something else! Not only was she pretty, but this girl had a head on her shoulders. But what sealed the deal for me, this girl loved Jesus, and she could spin a basketball on her finger! It sounds silly, but it was then that I thought, God, is this the girl you want me to marry? So I stepped out in faith, and married my new best friend! My wife Diane, was a blessing from the Lord!

Now if you were to have told me back then, that someday I would get married, have twelve children and travel the world with my family, I would have thought you were crazy! But that is exactly what started to happen. Not all at once, of course. But we just kept seeking the Lord and tried to be obedient to his call on our lives. Before we knew it, we were living in the country and had 3 little boys! I was working full time and also performing the Spin - tacular Basketball Show on the weekends.

Having a full time job was a blessing, but God kept prying my heart, and I felt called to do ministry full time. This was not just me, for God was speaking to Diane as well. We wanted to share God's message of Hope to our generation. We were already speaking in schools, camps, nursing homes, and any other place that would have us.

It was a step of faith, but as we would read the Bible, God was giving us promises that He was going to take care of us! One Scripture that I read said this, **"He who calls you is faithful, who also will do it. (I Thes. 5:24)**

When I read that verse, I realized that God will make a way. Instead of acting on our fears, we tried to train ourselves to live by faith, and not by sight. We stepped out in faith not knowing where our next meal was going to come from. It was a challenge, but God continues to be true to His promises in His Word.

SETTING A GUINNESS WORLD SPIN RECORD

"Hey, Bruce, I think you should try to set the world record for spinning the most basketballs." My friend Dan Horton said after a school assembly program in Kansas. Dan was a friend from Hiawatha, KS, and he had lined up some school assembly programs for me in the area.

"Dan, what is the current record?" I asked.

"Well, Bruce, according to the Guinness Book, I believe it is twelve basketballs spinning at the same time. After you get them all spinning, you have to keep them spinning for five seconds."

"Hey, I am doing more than that right now," I said.

Diane and I prayed about it and during the third year of our marriage, God opened the door for me to attempt to set a world record for spinning the most basketballs. It was a success as I spun 15 basketballs all at the same time! Over the next eight years, God opened the door for me to break that record another three times on three different television shows. Two of the shows *Live with Regis and Kathy*, and the *Today Show*, were both live broadcast television shows. Once again, God took me out of my comfort zone and was placing me in situations that I had to overcome the fear of failure. During both of the live shows, I could sense the peace of God, and I knew I wasn't alone!

The spinning basketball and the unicycle became a great tool to reach kids and adults with the message that they can become Champions in Life's Game! So God gave Diane and I a vision to start Champions Forever Ministries, Inc., a nonprofit ministry. It was our goal to "Forever Uplift the Name of Jesus Christ, The Champion of Our Faith". We wanted to reach people with the message that with God, they can become true Champions in the Game of Life! We were doing programs not only around the local area but were getting invitations from across the country. It was our goal to use all of our resources to share this message of hope to our generation!

THE GROWING FAMILY

As the family continued to grow, we incorporated them into The Spin-tacular Basketball show. We had four kids, five kids, six kids, seven, eight, nine, then ten. With each child, we were getting asked the usual questions, "Are you going to have any more?" and "Don't you know what is causing that?"

We bought unicycles for the kids, and they learned to ride. The Spin-tacular Basketball Show went from me doing a solo act, to a growing family act. Diane also learned to ride the unicycle, and the whole show went to the next level and took on a new dimension.

ATTEMPTING THE SPIN ENDURANCE WORLD RECORD

As any parent knows, sometimes your kids can challenge you to go above and beyond what you thought you could do! The year was 2005, and one day our kids were reading the *Guinness Book of Records*. They saw a record for spinning the basketball a finger for the longest time at three hours and fifty nine minutes. "Hey dad, don't you think you can break that record?" My daughter Katie asked.

"Well, Katie, I don't know. I have only spun the basketball for about an hour without stopping. I am pretty sure I could spin it for at least four hours, though. Maybe I should give it a try." I said with a bit of hesitation.

In my mind I thought I could spin the ball that long, but during my life of spinning basketballs, I had never spun one for longer than an hour. So her little question started a quest to break a record.

Diane and I prayed about it, and we decided to go for it and try to honor God at the same time. We called the record attempt, "Spin for Him", the "Him" being Jesus! We called our local Scheels Sporting Goods Store and asked if we could attempt to break the record in their store. The managers were all for it.

So on a cold February morning, we got all set up in their store. The store managers blocked off a large area and we had two video cameras set up, while a couple managers sat with us the whole time to witness and record the event.

For the record, after you get the ball spinning on your finger, you have to keep it going by tapping it on the side with the other hand. This tapping had to happen every five to ten seconds or the ball would fall off. My sons - Jacob, Caleb, and Isaiah - were going to attempt the record with me. We all started at noon. It was our goal to go for at least four hours.

My son Isaiah went for one hour and eight minutes, and my son Caleb went for one hour and sixteen minutes. For their age at the time, they both did a great job! Jacob and I kept pressing on! We went past the four hour mark, broke the record, and kept going! Jacob ended up spinning for eight hours and forty six minutes! He had broke the record with me!

The store was set to close at 9:00 P.M., so we spent the night in the store with a couple managers. When the store opened the next morning, the Lord had given me the strength to spin it all night. I was so tired from staying up all night and both of my arms were so tired that I could barely hold them up! By the grace of God I ended up spinning it for 22 hours and 12 minutes. I couldn't have done it without the Lord, and without the support of my best friend, Diane!

People ask me all the time, "Did you take a break to eat or got to the bathroom." Well, I did eat, and I did go the bathroom but the ball never

stopped spinning! I had to go number one twice, and number two once! To let you know, wiping was a challenge, but I like challenges! It was a great victory, and we gave God the credit for once again, His unseen hand made it all possible!

THE PRAYER OF ONE YOUNG GIRL

When we had ten children, they were made up of eight boys and two girls. My daughters, Katie and Hollie, were definitely out-numbered. Diane was three months pregnant with our eleventh child. One night my 10-year-old daughter, Hollie, came to me.

"Hey Dad, isn't it great that Mom is going to have another baby! I can hardly wait to see it!" Hollie said in anticipation.

"Yes Hollie, we are all looking forward to greeting the new member of the family, but Diane still has about six months to go, so we will just have to wait." I said.

"But Dad, you know, Katie and I are out-numbered in the family. I mean we have a lot of brothers. Wouldn't be great if mom had a baby girl?"

"Well, I wouldn't get my hopes up Hollie, because we do have eight boys, and the last four in a row --- Ben, Micah, Zach, and Nathan --- are all boys! I just know this next one is going to be a boy, too." I said.

"Hey Dad, I have a better plan! Wouldn't it be great if Mom had TWIN GIRLS! Then Katie and I would each have a little sister!" Hollie said in anticipation!

"Now Hollie, I don't want to burst your bubble, but that is asking a little too much. You will just have to accept the fact that you are going to be stuck with a lot of brothers. After all, twins don't run in the family."

"Well, you know what Dad, I am going to pray, and ask God for twin girls!" Hollie said with great assurance!

Six months later, I was talking to Diane, "You know honey, we have gone through ten pregnancies, and ten births, and I hate to say this to you, my lovely wife, but this is the biggest belly you've had yet!" I said in the most loving manner possible. "If I am standing next to you and you turn around, you about knock me over with you belly!"

"Yes, I know! When I was six months pregnant, I was ready for the baby to be born, but now that I am around nine months. I am really ready for this to happen!"

"Yeah, I am surprised that there are not twins in there. But our midwife assured us that it was just one big baby. Each time she checks you out, she can only hear one heartbeat, and she even let me listen. I only heard one heartbeat as well."

Later that evening at 12:30 A.M. on Nov. 6, 2008, Isaiah came running out to the shed, "Dad, mom's water broke!"

"Really? Oh, boy, here we go again! We will have to call the midwife." I said, knowing from experience the next order of events.

About two hours later, "Bruce, can you believe it! WE HAVE TWIN GIRLS! That was an amazingly quick birth!" Diane said as my daughter Katie held one baby and Caleb held the other one!

"Go wake up the rest of the kids and tell them the great news! Oh! Yeah, go tell Hollie that her prayer was answered!" I said excitedly.

After all the kids got up they came into our bedroom. "Hey Hollie, God answered your prayers! You got your twin sisters!" I said as she came in the room.

"Wow! Mom! You did it! I am so excited, Katie and I each have a sister!" Hollie said with excitement as she held one of the new girls.

153

"What shall we name them?" I asked as the kids gave their recommendations.

"Let's name them Tori and Tessa!" Came the consensus!

God had answered our prayers for a safe delivery, and we got the added bonus of having not one, but two beautiful little girls! I didn't think something like that would be possible, but never underestimate the power of prayer, even if it is coming from a young girl.

AMERICA'S GOT TALENT

We had been performing as a family for 20 years. All the kids had gotten really good at basketball tricks and also riding small and very tall unicycles! Our newest additions, - Ben, Micah, Zach, Nathan, Tori and Tessa - were also coming along very well. They were adding a new dimension to the show that I never dreamed possible!

In the summer of 2012, while doing prison ministry in Florida, a prisoner named Jamaal came up to me after I did a program.

"You know Bruce, I was really encouraged by the show today. Thanks for visiting us here in prison, and for sharing the good news of Jesus Christ! The hour that you did your show felt like I wasn't even in prison! Thanks so much! Also, I think you and our family should be on that show, *America's God Talent* (AGT). Your show is amazing, and I think all of America needs to see you guys."

"Yeah, I have had other people tell me that, but I don't know if it would work out." I said.

Then Jamaal grabbed me by the arm and said:

"Listen Bruce, you need to make the effort, because I know God will bless you, and you can share God's message with the world," He said with a serious tone.

When I got home, I talked to Diane about what Jamaal had said, and I thought, could God be speaking through a prisoner named Jamaal? To appease my conscience, I went to the AGT website, and submitted a video. We never heard back from them so we just forgot about it. Then in February of 2013, AGT called us up and asked us to come and audition in Chicago. They had seen our video and thought it would be a great fit. The only problem, they gave us three days to prepare and travel to Chicago! We rounded everyone up and drove the whole family out to Chicago.

When we showed up in Chicago there were 5000 people ready to audition on Saturday and 5000 on Sunday. In all about 75,000 other contestants from across the USA auditioned for the AGT producers in various cities.

We did a 90 second routine that included basketballs and very tall unicycles ranging in height from 5-feet to 10-feet tall. The producers loved what they saw, so they narrowed the 75,000 acts down to 400, and invited us to the next level.

DISASTER AFTER OUR FIRST AUDITION

After our first successful audition in Chicago with AGT, we drove into an ice storm on Interstate 90. We were driving our 45-foot, 20-ton converted MCI bus, and pulling our trailer. It was so slippery out. We had slowed down to 25 - 30 mph. As we came around a bend in the interstate, we were surprised by five vehicles that were stopped on the interstate. They were trying to move but because it was so slippery, they couldn't! It was surprising but one of the vehicles that was stranded by the ice was a snowplow. It was so slippery that even he couldn't drive. There was also a semi truck, a Class C motorhome,

and two cars. Three of them were on the right and two of them were on the road. Because of the curve in the road hidden by a train bridge, we didn't see them. There was a small path through the cars, and I tried to slow down but my back end slid to the right, toward the Class C motorhome, and BANG! The right side of our bus hit the whole left side of the motorhome! When we hit the motorhome, that pushed the back of our bus to the left, which made the front go to the right, and we were out of control. I drove it down the ditch where there was snow and ice. I didn't want to stop or let the bus slow down for fear of getting it stuck. So I sped up and kept driving for about 150-yards. Then I drove it back up the ditch and back onto the road! I couldn't believe it. We were back on the road! Our trailer broke off at impact and was in the ditch. Thankfully no one was hurt in our bus or the motorhome that we hit, but there was some extensive damage to side of our bus, and our trailer axles were bent.

We were able to drive the bus home but because of the bent axles on the trailer we had to go back the next day to retrieve our trailer from the towing company. I didn't have a truck or a trailer large enough so I called my friend Bret, "Bret, this is Bruce. I know you are busy with the Law Office, but I am in a bind. We got in an accident with our bus, and my cargo trailer is at a towing company a couple hours from here. I have some programs that I have to travel to in a few days, so could I use your truck and flatbed trailer to pick up our cargo trailer? I have to repair the trailer when I get it home." I explained.

"Yes you can use my trailer, Bruce. But better yet, I will come, pick you up and drive you over there, myself! Bret said.

Since the axles were bent, we had to put our trailer on Bret's larger flatbed trailer. When we got it home we were slowly pulling our trailer off the flatbed trailer. Josiah was helping to lift the cargo trailer hitch off the trailer as he did it fell and about 1/4 inch of the tip of his finger was chopped off. We literally went from being on such a high with making the next level with America's Got Talent, to trying to figure out what God was doing.

Diane and I got on our knees because it was a very difficult set of events. It says in Scripture to offer the sacrifice of praise. **"Therefore by Him let us continually offer the sacrifice of praise to God, that is the fruit of our lips, giving thanks to His name"** (Hebrews 13:15). It is easy to praise God when things are going well, but it is a sacrifice to praise God when things are not going well. With all the damage, and with part of Josiah's finger gone, it was difficult to praise God, but in obedience to Scripture, we stepped out in faith and did it anyway. We praised God because we were going to live by faith and not by sight!

Our bus was still drivable but needed cosmetic repairs. We had programs coming up that we were scheduled to do. In between programs, we spent the next month repairing our bus and our trailer, all the while Josiah's finger was healing. As I pondered our situation with AGT, I felt like God was saying, "Are you going to quit? Or are you going to press on?" In Isaiah 41:10, God says, **"Fear not, for I am with you; do not be dismayed, for I am your God. I will strengthen you, Yes, I will help you, I will uphold you with My righteous right hand."**

We continued to praise God for the good and the bad, knowing that God was in control. God comforted us with His Scriptures, and it was then that I felt that God was shifting my focus! He was speaking to my heart, that I needed to stop focusing on our problems and look at the possibilities and our purpose; Instead of focusing on our obstacles, focus on our opportunities, instead of dwelling on our difficulties, dwell on our destiny, and instead of being defeated by trials, then use our trials to became our testimonies!

God was opening up an opportunity for my family and I to testify to the grace and mercy of God through it all! We can say with confidence that it wasn't the talent of our family that got us where we were, it was the unseen hand of God working through the circumstances and in our lives. Did God do this because we were special people. No, He did it because He can, and He loves us. It was our prayer to walk in that Love!

PRESSING ON

Two months later, we were back in Chicago in front of 2000 people and the celebrity judges, who, at the time were Howard Stern, Howie Mandel, Heidi Klum, and Mel B. The Lord gave us favor with the judges. The judges narrowed the 400 acts down to just 100, and moved us to the next level.

ON TO LAS VEGAS

A month after Chicago, our whole family was in Las Vegas, at Planet Hollywood. We were once again standing in front of the same judges. God again gave us favor with the judges and the producers, and they narrowed the 100 acts down to the last 50. We couldn't believe it! We were included in the last 50 acts! We had made it to the finals of AGT, and it was all because an unknown prisoner from Florida grabbed my arm and encouraged me to GO FOR IT!

TO NEW YORK CITY AND THE FINALS OF AGT

We were scheduled to be performing at the world famous Radio City Music Hall in New York City, NY. I have heard that many singers and performers have dreamed of performing there, but I have to confess. It was never my dream or my family's dream to perform at Radio City Music Hall. I didn't even know that something like this was even possible in my life. Because of God's Divine Hand, and His open door, we had been prepared for the

task at hand. We were going to go through it, but not on our own strength, but on His strength. We were seeing great things on the horizon!

We were shocked by how quickly things changed. All of the sudden, word got out that we were in the finals of the super bowl of talent shows, and we were getting calls by the media from all over the local area.

We were scheduled to perform a 90 second routine on the stage at Radio City Music Hall. It was easy to think that it was just 90 seconds, but the preparation that had to be done for our family to perform for those 90 seconds was very difficult! Between the Las Vegas appearance and the New York City appearance, we had a month and a half. So we were practicing a whole new routine at the local high school gym close to where we

lived in Elkton, SD.

Because we didn't know what to expect when we were on the stage at Radio City, I wanted the family to prepare for the unexpected. Tal Farnum, a friend, coach and a teacher at Elkton High School in Elkton, SD, was kind enough to open the local gym for us so that we could practice. We would be on a restricted stage with dimmed lights or flashing lights. Tal had strobe lights, so we practiced our tall unicycle routine in the gym, without any lights on, except for the flashing strobe lights. While we were in New York, I didn't want any surprises, so we made our practicing conditions as bad or worse than they would be in New York on the stage.

In the month and half that we had to prepare, *AGT* sent out a crew to film our family in action at home. Many media outlets also came to our house as well. We were scheduling interviews with TV, radio and newspapers from all around the local area and the whole state.

On our earlier rounds with *AGT*, we had driven to Chicago twice and drove down to Las Vegas once. For the last round we decided to fly to New York. We have two sizes of unicycles in our show. Small ones that we got from (Unicycle.com - Just talk to Amy if you need one), and very large ones called Giraffe unicycles. The very large ones were the unicycles we were going to fly to New York with. Because of the very large size of the unicycles, it is difficult to find and buy them at a store. Also, riding very tall unicycles can be dangerous if you don't know what you are doing, so they don't sell these at Walmart!

That is why I am so thankful for my dad. He taught me how to weld when I was growing up. So with this passed down skill, I had to custom design and build each unicycle by hand. All of the giraffe unicycles are constructed of tig welded aluminum, and range in size from five-feet to ten-feet in height. As the saying goes, it takes twice the man to ride half the bike, and if you ever tried to ride a unicycle, you know that to be true!

To fly all of them to New York on a jet was a different story. We designed all of the unicycles to collapse into bags, but we didn't have enough bags for everyone. Eight of the unicycles were ten-footers, two of them were eight footers, one was a five-footer, and we had two small unicycles for Tori and Tessa. Plus we had two very small mini bicycles as well. In all we had fifteen pieces of equipment besides our personal luggage that had to fly to New York.

As you can imagine, if it is difficult to find unicycles this size it will be hard to find bags to fit them in. So we custom designed seven extra large roller bags to carry the extra unicycles. We spent a week just gathering materials, sewing, and making and preparing bags for all our equipment.

The Lord's timing for the final show was

perfect. Our youngest, the twins, Tori & Tessa, were 4 at the time, and both of them had just learned how to ride a unicycle in time for the final show. We called them our "Secret Weapon". For the planned routine, we were going to start and end the show with these two.

Three weeks prior to the big trip to New York, I called up my friend Caz McCaslin, the CEO of Upward Sports in South Carolina.

"Hey Caz! This is Bruce. You aren't going to believe this, but my family and I are in the finals of America's Got Talent!

"Bruce! That's Great brother! Actually we have been following your progress. Leslie and I will be praying for you guys, but hey, here's an idea, maybe we can fly to New York, so we can come and help you with all the kids." Caz said.

"Seriously, Caz! Wow! That would be awesome, and the kids would love it!" I said with expectation.

Three weeks later, the whole family flew to New York.

We were picked up in limo buses and brought to the downtown Hilton which was just a few blocks from Radio City Music Hall. We were scheduled to be there for 8 days before our scheduled appearance so we could prepare for the show. Caz, his wife Leslie, and their daughter Mary Caroline, stayed with us at the Hilton. They were a huge help to us with all the kids, and getting things carried here and there, and Caz was even backstage helping us get on our unicycles! In all it was an awesome time!

We spent the week getting fitted for the uniforms for our routine, and practicing our routine at a local college gymnasium. We also practiced four different times on the main stage at Radio City Music Hall. It was now the day of the show, and we were getting all of our stuff ready.

When we were back stage getting prepared for our 90 second routine, I was reminded of all the years of practice, the thousands of miles of travel, the hundreds of performances, the successes, the failures, the frustrations, the fear, falling down, getting up, chasing basketballs, and everything else that led us to this point. I couldn't help but give thanks to God, not only for the many opportunities, but also for the struggles. For it was the struggles that built our faith, endurance and strength.

FINAL MOMENTS BACKSTAGE

Diane and I called the family together backstage for our final prayer before we took the stage. After we said a prayer, I looked into the eyes of each family member. I could barely contain myself, and I said, "God has brought us here for a reason, and that reason is not about us, it is to honor HIM! Diane and I love each of you so much, and we are honored to have you as our children. Thank you for being such a blessing to us. We have overcome a lot to be here, and tonight, God is giving you the opportunity to be a blessing to the whole world! You have done what it takes to be here. With the gift God has given you, go do what you

do best! Have fun, and give all the honor to the One who has made it all possible. One more thing, try not to focus on the millions who will be watching just do your best for the audience of ONE!"

SHOW TIME

We got onto our unicycles and waited for our music to start. AGT had 16 cameras that would be recording our effort, and everything was now on the line.

Our music started, and our 90 second routine to "WOW" America was off and running. Everything seemed like a slow-motion blur. We had tweaked and practiced our routine so much, we really didn't have to think about it, for it had become second nature. Because of the bright stage lights, we couldn't see the 5000 people in the Radio City Music Hall audience, but we could hear the thunderous applause on introduction, and the many cheers, Oooo's and ahhhh's in the background.

Our routine went flawless! The kids did great, and the AGT Producers even had fireworks at the end of our performance! The Radio City crowd loved the show, and we were the only group that got two, yes two standing ovations! A couple of judges for some reason didn't find us too favorable, and the crowd booed them for their comments, but for us, it was a victory. God had given us everything we needed to overcome, to prosper, and to succeed! Everything went just like we prayed and practiced! It was perfect, and we were praising the Lord!

People ask, what was it like preparing for, and performing in front of 20 million people on the biggest stage on television? Well just imagine trying to run, jump, ride, spin, dribble, lift, pack, unpack, clean, carry, eat & sleep all at the same time, while you are trying to swim. That's a little of what it was like! Even though it was challenging, it was an incredible experience.

APPLICATION:
HOW TO BECOME AN OVERCOMER

As the stories have related, life can be full of challenges and problems. Have you ever had a problem, trial, or a temptation that you struggled with, only to wake up a little later to the remorseful fact that you had slipped and failed to overcome? Or perhaps you are struggling with some habit that holds you as its slave. You struggle, wrestle, always trying to fight it, yet somehow you are never able to conquer it. Maybe you have some sin or some weakness, perhaps it is a secret sin, you have been unable to overcome? Why are we not more successful in living up to God's standard? Why do we slip and fall occasionally? It is because we have our focus wrong.

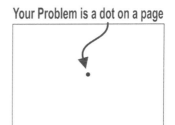

Your Problem is a dot on a page

The devil wants you to get your eyes off of God, and onto your problem. In relation to how God sees your problem, it is nothing but a dot on a piece of paper. When you see things from God's perspective, every difficulty looks in focus and manageable. But the devil will hand you the Magnifying Glass of Fear. Now all of the sudden, your dot on the page just got bigger. Oh, oh, that seemingly manageable problem has just grown! If that isn't bad enough, while you are so occupied and focused on your growing problem, you are

Magnifying Glass of FEAR
Your Problem just got BIGGER!

Microscope of FEAR
Your Problem Covers the page

then handed the Microscope of FEAR!

Your growing problem has just become the focus of your entire life. What you thought was just a dot on the page, the devil has convinced you that it is the whole page! Now it is difficult to do or think about anything else. The devil has you so focused on the problem, you have lost sight of the solution. Did the dot actually grow, or did it appear to grow?

The word **FEAR** stands for **False Evidence Appearing Real**! To be an Overcomer, Jesus wants us to get our life in focus and abide in Him and not focus on all the False Evidence! Here is how YOU can overcome where you are weakest and hardest tempted!

OVERCOMING THE GIANT

Zig Ziggler, the motivational speaker once said, **"Success comes, when opportunity meets preparation."** When we were on *America's Got Talent*, my family and I had been preparing for our opportunity to do this 90 second routine for six months. But in reality, God had been preparing my whole family and me for this moment ever since I learned how to spin a basketball and ride a unicycle.

Scripture talks about being faithful in little things, and this became true in my life. In an average life, big opportunities rarely come if ever, but the little opportunities are all around us. A large building doesn't just happen overnight, but it can be slowly built one brick at a time. As I began to ponder the different experiences both good and bad, that had brought us to our time on *AGT*, it reminded me of one of my favorite bible stories, the story of David and Goliath.

Right before David confronted Goliath, he had to convince King Saul that he was the man for the job. Why was David the man for the job? Because God had already prepared David for this task! King Saul didn't know about what David had done, but God knew, and God was about to show the whole world that it was He who gives the victory! David actually had been trained as a warrior for this mission of killing a Giant while tending sheep:

"But David said to Saul, 'Your servant used to keep his father's sheep, and when a lion or a bear came and took a lamb out of the flock, I went out after it and struck it, and delivered the lamb from its mouth; and when it arose against me, I caught it by its beard, and struck and killed it. Your servant has killed both lion and bear; and this uncircumcised Philistine will be like one of them, seeing he has defied the armies of the living God'" (I Samuel 17:34-36).

GOD BRINGS DANGER DAVID'S WAY

While David was tending his father's sheep, his older brothers went off to war. David was left at home to do a seemingly insignificant task of tending sheep. While tending those sheep, at times, I am sure it was boring. But in obedience to his parents, he did his job. David's success came when his preparation met his opportunity. While watching sheep, I am sure he had some free time to practice such skills as slinging a stone at a tree, or maybe his skill with a knife, or playing his harp. You see, while watching those boring sheep, God separated David and was planting him to grow into an overcomer. During this time, God had orchestrated two dangerous events to come David's way. At two different times, a lion and a bear attacked the sheep! To protect the sheep, David killed them both! God had delivered both the lion and the bear into David's hand for protection of the sheep. But God had a greater purpose for this danger. David was just doing his job of protecting the sheep, but God was preparing David for a larger battle with higher stakes.

DAVID SHOWED COURAGE

Courage is not the absence of fear, but rather, with God's strength, facing our fears. I am sure that David was fearful when he was facing both the lion and the bear, but David was able to overcome and kill both animals with the confidence and strength that God gave him. It was this struggle that gave him the courage to challenge Goliath.

If you notice, David said that it was God who delivered the lion and bear into his hand, and not his own strength. Because he was faithful with the sheep, in overcoming when nobody was watching, he was able to overcome when everyone was watching. Protecting the sheep was his defining moment, slaying Goliath was his destiny moment.

As David was approaching Goliath, the giant was shouting at David, attempting to discourage and show David how feeble he was. Because David knew his standing with God, that he was God's child, David knew that the victory did not reside with Goliath, but with God. So even though David saw the immense size of the Giant, that was not his focus. His focus was on the God who had delivered him from the lion and the bear. All the other warriors in Israel's army had the microscope

Isaiah and Katie in Israel at King David's Tomb

of fear. All they could see was the problem and not the solution. David on the other hand, saw Goliath for what he was. **In relation to God, Goliath was just a dot on the page!** Goliath in his pride, only saw a feeble young lad and didn't know that this young man was a seasoned warrior. David was going to walk into his destiny.

TO OVERCOME, YOU MUST CONFESS IT

Words are powerful! In 1 Samuel 17, as David approached giant, Goliath confessed to David what he was going to do to him: **"I am going to feed your flesh to the birds of the air and the beasts of the field"**. Then David countered that confession with his own confession based not on his own strength, but on God's: **"You come at me with sword and spear, and with a javelin. But I come to you in the Name of the Lord of Hosts, the God of the armies of Israel whom you have defied. This day the Lord will deliver you into my hand, and I will strike you and take your head from you."**

THE BEST PART OF DAVID AND GOLIATH

The best part of this story is what happens next. **"So it was, when the Philistine arose and came and drew near to meet David, that David hurried and ran toward the army to meet the Philistine"** (1 Sam 17:48). David didn't wait for the giant to approach him, it says that **he RAN at the giant!** When you are walking in the strength of the Lord, it gives you confidence beyond your years and beyond your strength! David did not shy away from the problem, but he ran at the problem with all his might! **The best way to get rid of a problem, is to solve it!** David's confrontation with Goliath was the turning point for David and also the nation of Israel! With one sling of the stone, and one chop of the sword, David went from a nobody to a somebody! David solved his problem and Israel's problem. He became the most famous warrior in the history of the nation.

A LESSON FROM JESUS, THE OVERCOMER

Even Jesus, the Son of God, had problems, obstacles, temptations and trials to overcome. He had to overcome many of the same things that are plaguing us. At the cross, he defeated sin, death, and the devil. Jesus was not just an Overcomer He was THE OVERCOMER.

The last words of a person are usually some of the most important words spoken. If the last words are repeated, then they must be SUPER IMPORTANT! In the last book of the Bible, the book of Revelation, we have some of Jesus' last words. In Revelation chapters two & three, Jesus repeats this phrase seven times: "To him who Overcomes". The fact that Jesus repeats this phrase seven times in the course of two chapters in the last book of the Bible is a good indication that these are very important words! Apparently Jesus wants us to be overcomers.

You just read about some struggles that my family and I have had to overcome in life's journey. Also, you read about David overcoming the Giant. At this moment, you may have a Giant in your life that needs overcoming! It might be some addiction, sin, problem or struggle. Your problem may be more than you can bear. But there is hope!

Revelation 12:11 says: **"And they overcame by the blood of the Lamb and by the word of their testimony."** If you want to be an overcomer, there are two steps according to this verse. Those two things are: "the blood of the Lamb", and the "word of their testimony".

Jesus' blood was the purchase price for victory. In other words the debt was paid, so we have already won! We can walk in that victory.

The second thing to remember is that our words are powerful! Remember the confession of David against Goliath. He confessed to God, to Goliath, and to himself the desired outcome! Why did his confession work and Goliath's didn't? Because David was obeying God, and

Goliath wasn't. According to Deuteronomy chapter 28, when you obey God's voice, the blessing of God will come upon you and overtake you. One of the blessings listed in Deuteronomy 28, is the defeat of enemies!

If you want to be an overcomer, just be like Jesus. What was Jesus like? When you study the life of Jesus, you will find several important characteristics about his life that caused Him to overcome sin, death, and Satan:

1) He spent much time in prayer, but He never spoke the problem. He always prayed and spoke the answer from the Word of God.
2) He always spoke the end results, and never what He saw or felt.
3) He used the written word to defeat Satan.

SCIENCE CONFIRMS WHAT THE BIBLE SAYS

Pastor Mark Hankins sheds light on some information that will be life changing:

"A leading neurosurgeon has said that the speech center in the brain exercises dominion over the whole central nervous system. He also stated that this is a recent discovery. He said that you can cause different parts of the body to respond with stimuli to corresponding parts of the human brain. However when the speech center is stimulated, the entire central nervous system responds. This means that when anyone says, "I am weak," the speech center sends out the message to the whole body to prepare to be weak. This must be the reason God said, 'Let the weak say, I am strong,' Joel 3:10."

*From: "The Speech Center Exercises Dominion" by Mark Hankins

Paul confesses to us in Romans chapter 7 that even he had a terrible struggle with sin. He tells us that the good things that he knows he should do, he doesn't

do, and the evil things that he knows that he shouldn't do, he does. He comes to the conclusion that the only way that he will ever be delivered from his body of sin and death, was through Jesus Christ.

Paul also wrote **"I beseech you therefore, brethren, by the mercies of God, that you present your bodies a living sacrifice, holy, acceptable to God, which is your reasonable service. And do not be conformed to this world, but be transformed by the renewing of your mind, that you may prove what is that good and acceptable and perfect will of God" (Romans 12:1-2).**

God wants us to offer our bodies as "a living sacrifice, holy, acceptable to God, which is your reasonable service". Because of what God has done for us, the least we can do for Him is present our bodies a living sacrifice.

In the Old Testament, the priests used to kill the animal, put the sacrifice on the alter, then burn the sacrifice. If you notice in Romans 12, God doesn't want a dead animal to be sacrificed on the alter, He wants YOU! There is one problem with a living sacrifice. A LIVING sacrifice has the ability to crawl off the alter. We may be enthusiastic about becoming this Living Sacrifice for Jesus, so we crawl onto that alter with confidence. But as we are up there, the heat gets turned up and we smell something burning. It is then that we realize that it is our flesh getting cooked.

When you renew you mind in God's Word, you will find out who you are in the eyes of God, and it will give you the strength and the confidence to confront the giant in your life with enthusiasm.

To be a Champion, you have to start 1) Thinking like a Champion, 2) Talking like a Champion, and 3) Acting like a Champion!

Code #6

CHAMPIONS SHOW LOVE BY GIVING OF THEIR TIME, TALENT AND FINANCES TO GOD AND TO OTHERS.

"Command those who are rich in this present age not to be haughty, nor to trust in uncertain riches but in the living God, who gives us richly all things to enjoy. Let them do good, that they be rich in good works, ready to give, willing to share, storing up for themselves a good foundation for the time to come, that they may lay hold on eternal life" (1 Timothy 6:17-19).

"Give, and it will be given to you: good measure, pressed down, shaken together, and running over will be put into your bosom. For with the same measure that you use, it will be measured back to you" (Luke 6:38).

"How do you spell LOVE? L-O-V-E, right? Wrong You spell it T-I-M-E! The greatest gift you can give someone, is your time. When you dedicate your time to others, you are truly loving others, and offering a part of yourself that you will never get back."
Anonymous

All love comes from God, and all true Champions show their love by giving love back to God and giving God's love to others. Scripture says that God is not just a giver, He is THEE GIVER! As you walk with God, the fruit that you see is that you will want to be a giver as well. **But I must warn you You cannot out-give God. I will say that again. YOU CANNOT OUT-GIVE GOD! HOW ABOUT A THIRD TIME! YOU CANNOT OUT-GIVE GOD!**

We know this from experience because my family and I have actually experienced the overwhelming giving heart of God. To set the stage and to show you how God worked, I am going to share a story with you that has to do with my wife, Diane, our children, my younger sister, Janine, and Pastor John Chavez from California. This story starts when I was a little kid, and had a best friend.

STORY:
MUD ON THE WALL

It was fun growing up in a large family. There are 12 children in the family that I came from and being the 11th of 12 children, I had ten older siblings and one younger sister. My mother and father loved their children and gave us a good foundation, for this love has stood the test of time. To this day, our family is very close.

My younger sister, Janine, also known as Beanie, is one year younger than me and being the two youngest in a large family, my sister Janine and I did everything together. We played together, had fun together, and got into trouble together. Even though Janine was a girl, she was tougher than most boys that I knew. During our growing up years on our farm near Jefferson, SD, she was my best friend.

Being raised on a farm afforded opportunities for adventure, and Janine, who was six-years-old at the time and I, being seven, did a lot of exploring.

One day, we were in the house and looked outside. It rained about 2 inches the night before, and there were mud puddles all over our gravel driveway.

Like most kids, we both loved playing in the mud. It was especially good after a rain!

"Hey Beanie, do you want to go outside and play in the mud?" I said to my little sister Janine, as we looked out the window of our living room?

"Yeah, Bruce, that sounds like fun!" Janine said as we proceeded to get ourselves ready.

A few minutes later, we found ourselves in our bare feet sloshing through the puddles.

Next to our house, we had an unattached garage where my dad kept a lot of his tools. He spent a lot of time working on farm projects or fixing things in that garage and he had recently repainted the outside of the garage an attractive bright white. In front of the garage, was our gravel driveway with a large mud puddle, and that's where our adventure began.

Beanie and I loved making mud pies, and we found that if we dug our hands through the puddle; then through the top layer of gravel; that we could get to the smooth, gooey black mud! So we dug down and started to make some mud pies. After we made three mud pies, we carefully place them on the ground so they could dry.

As I was digging in the mud getting ready to make my next mud pie, my attention was drawn to the beautifully painted white wall of the garage.

"Hey Beanie, I wonder what a mud pie would look like on the white garage?" I said as I dug deep in the mud.

"I don't know, Brucey, why don't you put a big mud pie on it and find out." Beanie replied with a big smile.

Man, I loved my little sister, especially when she encouraged me in new adventures like this! When she gave me the green light to do the fun stuff, it made having a little sister all the more fun!

Ten seconds later, I was standing in front of the outside wall of my dad's nice white garage, with the biggest scoop of mud that my two little hands could muster.

"I wonder where I should put it," I said to myself as I looked at the large garage wall.

The middle looked like the best place, so I proceeded to mash that big pile of mud with my right hand onto the side wall of the garage.

As a little kid, I really don't know what was motivating me other than the fact that it just plain looked like fun! The garage looked so white, and the mud looked so black, that I felt like an artist making a painting on a canvas, and this would be my mud-ster-piece, I mean masterpiece. But this seemingly innocent action would have repercussions later in the day, as you will soon see.

After a half hour of making more mud pies, splashing in the water, and wading through all the mud puddles, we were finished. The hot sun was through the clouds, and everything was drying up, including our newly made mud pies! Even my masterpiece on the side of the garage was drying up and looking good.

Later that afternoon, Beanie and I forgot about our mud pies and joined our older siblings, Ann and Bert. We all headed to the end of our driveway for our daily routine. It was our custom to go to the end of our driveway, sit down on the grass, and wait for our dad to come home from work.

Along with farming, my dad, Ray, worked at the WJ Company in Sioux City, Iowa, about a 25 minute drive from our home. This company sold roofing and insulation supplies to contractors in the area. Because my dad had many mouths to feed, he not only farmed near Jefferson, SD, he had to supplement his income by working in Sioux City to make ends meet for the family.

After sitting there for about 10 minutes, in the distance we could see dad's green Ford pickup truck coming down the road. This always made us excited. As dad rounded the corner of the driveway, Beanie and I were jumping up and down. He stopped the truck, reached over and opened the door, and asked, "Do you guys need a ride?"

"Yes dad, Yippee!" We all squealed in unison.

So all four of us jumped in for the short 50 yard ride. Even though it was brief, this little daily ritual made us feel so special. Dad was as glad to see us, as we were to see him.

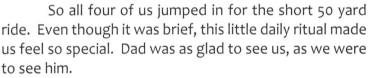

As we stopped the truck and jumped out, I ran over gave dad a hug and after the hug, he and I had a little routine that we would do. He would back up a few steps, put his arms in front of his face for protection, and dad and I would do a little slap boxing! When my dad was younger, he used to be a boxer. When he would get home from work, he would box both my brother Bert and me for a few seconds. With his hands up in the boxing position, he would give me a quick slap tap to the face. Not hard enough to hurt, but hard enough to make you put your hands up for protection. I would then try to return the favor, by giving him a return slap, but I could never get him.

One time we were really going at it, and I accidentally punched my dad in the stomach and knocked the wind out of him! Beings I was only seven at the time, it took him by surprise, and he was trying to laugh and catch his breath at the same time. From that moment on, dad would watch out for those low jabs! This little boxing routine would go on for about 10 seconds, after this, my dad would grab us, one at a time, under our arms and then would twist us around and flip us up on one of his shoulders. Dad was strong, and it was fun getting tossed up on his shoulder. In all, this routine took less than three or four minutes, but it never got old! When we were done, we all started to head into the house.

As we were walking to the house, I could see my dad smiling as he looked at his newly painted garage. But his smile soon faded as he walked closer and looked over to the middle of the garage wall. The large mud pie on the garage had dried, and dad was looking right at my creation! By this time, I had totally forgot about our mud pie creations, but my memory was quickly recalling my time with Beanie!

"Hey, who put mud on the garage?" Dad said with a stern voice.

My "masterpiece" had turned into "mischief". We all heard Dad's tone, and it didn't sound good. Bert, Ann, Janine and I, just went from having fun with dad, to "GET ME OUTTA HERE!"

When my little sister Janine heard dad's tone, she took off in a sprint to the house! Yes, she was the one who encouraged me in this crime. Sure, it was my idea, but her enthusiastic encouragement pushed me over the edge! I would have run with her, but it was too late, for dad was looking right at us! My best friend was gone, and I was left holding the bag! I was trapped! For me to run, would prove my guilt, and as I waited, dad was now interrogating the potential criminals.

My brother Bert, noticing dad's tone, immediately said, "Dad, I didn't do that!"

My sister Ann followed Bert's lead and said, "Well

dad, I didn't do it!"

Wow, they both told the truth, and now it was my turn to give a response. What was I going to say? Dad had a mean scowl on his face and did not look too happy. If I tell him that I did it, I will be in big trouble! Maybe I will just say "I didn't do it", and he will just forget about it. So being scared and red faced, I let out the biggest lie ever, in my short seven-year life span.

"Well um, I didn't do it, either!" I said as I looked at Bert and Ann, and choked up a gulp!

Dad looked at all three of us and from his actions, he knew one of us had done it, so he started to head into the house.

Great! He forgot about it! I thought as we all started following him as he walked toward the house.

Then he stopped us and said, "Hey, where are you guys going? Oh, NO! I am going to go in and get cleaned up for supper. But you guys are going to stay out here and will not get to come into the house until you figure out which one of you did it!" Dad said with his stern voice.

Wow! My little mind was in turmoil, for I was the cause of all this commotion. It was me who had done this dastardly act. Why did I do such a stupid thing. It did look messy, and at the time, I didn't realize that it would offend dad, but after doing the mud, and then lying to him, the muddy mess was getting even messier! If I told him the truth now, he would not only be mad at me for the mud, but he would be mad at me for telling a lie! I felt trapped!

So as dad went into the house, I could see Bert and Ann looking at me as they got closer to the mud spot. I started to walk little closer as well, but then I stopped when I noticed that right in the middle of the mud spot, was the condemning evidence. I didn't see it before, BUT THERE IT WAS! There was a perfectly made hand print, hard as a rock, baked by the sun for everyone

to see. What was I going to do?

I saw Bert walking closer to the garage to get a closer look at it.

"Hey you guys! There is a hand print right in the middle of this mud pie!" He said as he started putting his hand up to it.

As his hand was up to the print, he was measuring to see if his hand fit the print in the mud. Bert was 5-years older than me, and his hand was much too large for the print. Ann did the same thing. She was 2-years older and even though her hand was closer to my size, it was larger than the print as well.

Bert looked at me and said, "Bruce, weren't you and Janine playing over here earlier today? Get over here and put your hand up there."

I had learned over the years, that I better listen to my big brother. He not only was bigger than me, but a lot stronger as well and had proved it to me many times! If I put my hand there, I knew that my fate was sealed for sure, for my hand was going to fit like a glove. If I didn't put my hand there, then he would assume the print was mine because I couldn't prove otherwise. As I made my way over to the mud spot, Bert stopped me!

"Hey Bruce, LOOK! There is dried mud on your hand!" Bert said with a fierce tone.

Not only was my little hand going to fit like a glove, the mud on my hand was just more evidence that was closing in on me! By this time, my little mind was racing, thinking of a way to get out of this mess.

As I tried to brush the dried mud off my hand, an idea shot into my head. If I bent my fingers a little bit and put my palm below the palm on the print, then my fingers would appear smaller than the mold. I quickly placed my hand on the print for just a second, and tried to make my hand look too small.

"See, my hand is too little!" I said with a phony sense of relief.

Bert and Ann didn't seem to be buying my lies, and by this time, my little heart was aching. The first lie had led to another and even though I was guilty, I was desperately searching for a way out of my predicament without having to admit my fault.

My brother and sister were missing out on their supper because of me, and they continued to miss out as long as I was being a little hard head.

For the next few minutes, we stood there, looking at the mud, and looking at each other, looking at the mud, and looking at each other. Even though I tried to get it all off, there was still dried mud on the sides of my hands.

As thoughts continued to race through my mind, ten minutes passed but it seemed like forever. My dad finally came out the back door of the house, and called us over.

"Well, have you decided who did it?" He said with a firm look.

To which my brother Bert replied, "Dad, I didn't do it!"

Ann replied, "I didn't do it either, Dad."

Then, there was a slight pause. I looked at the mud on the garage and my dirty hands, and then I looked at Bert and Ann. Finally, I looked at dad and by this time, I was welling up with tears and started to cry. So I ran toward dad, gave him a hug, and said, "Dad, I did it!"

Dad looked at me, hugged me back and said, "Bruce, I figured you did it when I first saw the mud on the garage. I gave you a chance to be truthful, but you told me a lie. You made everyone wait for their supper. Thanks for telling me the truth. The mud is no big deal, but please don't do that again. I spent time and money making the garage look good, and you didn't help matters by putting that mud on the wall, and lying about it. I continued to cry, and hug dad and I said, "I am sorry, dad."

As I was hugging dad, he was patting my back, comforting me. Then dad looked at the mud and said to my older brother Bert, "Bert, go get the water hose and clean that off the garage."

Bert was kind enough to clean it up for me. What a nice brother!

Even though Janine ditched me in my muddy predicament, I learned a valuable lesson on telling the truth. Janine, was a great companion through my grade school and high school years. Later in college, she was the one who encouraged me to get to know Diane. Little did I know, Diane would later become my future bride, my new best friend, and the mother to our 12 children!

GOD'S MIRACLE PLAN OF ECONOMY

Fast forward the story to the early 1990's. My sister Janine was a teacher at Dakota Valley School. After graduating from college, Janine gave her time to helping our aging mom and dad. Mom and dad were in their late 60's, so Janine put off marriage to be with them after all the other kids moved out. Because she gave her time to honor our parents, I knew that God was going to bless her. Both of our parents eventually passed away so Janine moved near us here in Elkton, SD.

During this time, Diane, our kids and I were attending a Christian revival meeting organized by my sister Karen and her husband Steve. At this meeting, there was a man named Pastor John Chavez, from California. He was preaching and sharing his testimony about how God had provided for him and his ministry. He said, "If you are about the King's business, the King will be about your business! If you need a miracle in your life, you sometimes need to be a miracle in the life of another person!"

Some of the stories that Pastor Chavez was sharing were amazing. You could sense the Spirit of God speaking through him. As he spoke of his experiences, I felt the Spirit of God prompting me to take my spiritual life with Jesus to a new level. He shared a story about how he prayed to God for healing, and God healed him of a disease. He also prayed about being able to travel around and share the good news of Jesus Christ, but he needed wheels. He said that the King's business is seeking and saving souls. God helped him because out of the blue, a man gave him a $30,000 motorhome.

When I heard that, I thought, Just wait a second! What? Wow! Some guy just gave him a motorhome worth $30,000! How does that happen?

It was an amazing thought, for he had the motor home with him as proof! I kept thinking, What kind of person do you have to be for that to happen to you, and what kind of a person gives something like that? For someone to just up and give you a $30,000 motorhome, this Pastor Chavez must have a connection to God!

I was trying to wrap my head around the fact what somebody did that for this guy. On the outside, this Pastor didn't look that special, but I could tell that he had a heart to serve God.

Anyway, that really inspired my wife and I, and we decided that if we had the opportunity, we were going to be like the guy who gave that motorhome to Pastor Chavez. If there was someone who needed a miracle, then we were going to try to be a miracle for that person. We filed our experience with Pastor Chavez in our minds and didn't know who, what or how.

As Diane and I had been traveling and working, we had saved up about $5000 to put toward a new van since we were in need of an upgrade. While we were saving up, my sister Janine had a small car that needed repairing. Her car went into the shop, but we later found out that her car was not repairable. The engine was shot, and to try to fix it would not be worth it. So now she didn't have a car.

"Bruce, did you know your sister's car can't be

fixed?" Diane said to me one night.

"Yeah, I heard. That is too bad. Does she have any plans?" I said.

"Well, she doesn't have enough money for it right now, so she is going to have to try to save up." Diane said.

As we were thinking about Janine's plight, God spoke to both of our hearts. "You know Bruce, I really feel that even though we can't really afford it, we do have some money saved and maybe we should try to bless Janine." Diane said.

"Yes, Honey, I agree, and remember, 'If you need a miracle, you sometimes need to be a miracle for someone else.' Someday we may need a miracle, and it would be great to be miracle for her!" I said in agreement.

Since Janine did not have a car it was a difficult time for her, so we decided that we were going to try to find Janine a good used car, and use our savings to try to buy it. We wanted to do this as a surprise, so we didn't tell her.

We headed to Sioux Falls, SD, in search of a car for Janine. We were praying that God would lead us to the right one. After driving to many used car lots, we found a beautiful blue little Ford car with front wheel drive. It was a great car that was about five years old and had 40,000 miles on it. The price tag was $4500 so we stepped out in faith and purchased the car. After we purchased the car, we drove it home. At this time, Janine was out of town and was flying in from Indiana where she stayed with some friends for the week. To pick her up, we drove the car to the airport in Sioux Falls, SD. We met her at that baggage claim.

"Hey Beanie!" Diane said.

"Hey Diane, hi Bruce!" Janine replied.

"Did you have a good time in Indiana with your friends?" Diane asked.

"Yes, I did! Thanks for coming to pick me up."

"Hey Janine, Diane and I just got a new car!" I said as we walked toward the curb.

"Yeah, Janine, it drives really nice." Diane added.

"Oh Wow! That is a really nice car!" Janine responded.

At this point, we loaded her stuff in the back, and proceeded to get into the car.

"Wait, Janine, do you want to drive it?" I asked her as she was headed to one of the passenger doors.

"Oh, no, it is your car, I want you to drive it."

"But I would like you to drive it, Janine." I said.

"Yeah, Janine, we want you to drive it." Diane said in agreement.

"Ok, ok, twist my arm, ha ha ha!" She said as she made her way around to the drivers door.

As we pulled out of the airport she was loving the little car.

"Bruce and Diane, this little car is great! I am so happy for you guys! If you could, pray for me, because I need to get something like this. I just don't have the money right now, but I am believing that God will provide for me."

"Yes, Janine, as a matter of fact, I think God has already answered your prayer, because this car is not ours! This car is for YOU!" Diane said.

At that moment, Janine took her eyes off the road, and looked right at us, and said, "What? What did you say?"

"This car is for YOU, Janine!" Diane said, "God put it on our hearts to bless you with this car!"

At that moment, Janine started to cry and had to pull onto the shoulder of the road because she was crying. This made both Diane and me cry as well. As we all were crying, I was reminded of the Scriptures that say it is more blessed to give than it is to receive. As we were all crying, we said a prayer to the Lord and thanked him for allowing us to be a small part of the miracle in her life. Because of the blessing of being able to give, God continued to bless us and gave us miracles in return.

IF YOU ARE ABOUT THE KING'S BUSINESS, HE WILL BE ABOUT YOUR BUSINESS

The opportunities to share the basketball show were expanding. We were sharing a motivational message in the schools and other events and sharing the Gospel message of hope when we had opportunity. God was blessings us with invitations from all over the country and because we wanted to keep our family together, we would drive as much as we could. It was our goal to be a miracle in our generation.

As our family grew, we had to continually change to larger vehicles. Up to that point, here is a breakdown of what vehicles we had gone through. We started out by driving a small Honda hatchback. We went through three Honda cars; four Minivans; four 15 Passenger vans; and two Class C motorhomes.

The year was 2003, and during this time, we were driving a 32-foot Class C motorhome to all our programs. It worked well, but because we were putting thousands of miles on it, we were having maintenance issues. We decided to look for an upgrade. Something larger that had a diesel engine. We had bought those Class C motorhomes from a dealership in Mitchell, SD, and the Lord laid it on my heart to call the owner of the dealership to see about trading our motorhome in for a decent deal on an upgrade.

"Hi Doug. Yes, this is Bruce Crevier. My family and I have purchased a couple Class C motorhomes from you. Anyway, we are looking to trade our Class C motorhome in for Class A diesel pusher. Maybe something larger than what we have now, that has low miles, and that is not too old. If you could keep your eye out for a good deal on something like that since we have a limited budget, we would really appreciate it." I said.

"Well, we will look around to see if there are any trades coming in and see if there is anything like that available," Doug said as we hung up the phone.

After the first month, I never heard back from Doug. Then the second month went by and now we were into the third month. I just figured either he didn't find anything or he probably forgot about it. Then one day, Doug called me back.

"Hi Bruce. Yes, we talked a while back. I want to let you know, that I found a diesel Class A Travel Supreme on our lot that you should come and look at." Doug said.

"OK, Doug. Thanks for the tip. We will try to come over there tomorrow to check it out." I said as we hung up the phone.

Diane and I drove the two hours to Mitchell, SD, and he showed us the Travel Supreme 36-foot Class A diesel pusher. It was only two-years-old and had only 14,000 miles on it. It looked great, and when we drove it, we liked it even more. But the only problem, it had a price tag on it of $129,000, which was way out of our price range. There was no way we would be able to afford that. The cost was about three times what we paid for the Class C motorhomes, and we still had about $20,000 left to pay on the motorhome we were currently driving.

We took this Class A motorhome for a drive, and it handled great! With our growing family, it was definitely something that we needed and would have worked out well. But when we came back into the dealership lot, we had to give Doug the bad news.

"Doug, thanks so much for showing us this motor home, it is really nice and would work well for what we are trying to accomplish with our ministry, but we have a problem." I said.

"Yes Doug, we appreciate you showing us the motorhome. The problem we have, it is way our of our price range and we just can't afford it." Diane said as I

189

nodded in agreement.

Doug looked at us, and then said something totally unexpected, "Well, Bruce and Diane, I understand your situation, but that is not your problem, that is our problem, because we want to give it to you." Doug said.

At this moment, Diane looked at me with the same look that I gave her "Did he just say what I thought he said?"

I didn't want to ask him about what he just said because I was shocked and didn't know what to say at this point. But the more we talked to him, the more it was becoming quite clear. This guy, and this dealership were going to give our ministry this $129,000 motorhome.

"Doug, we don't know what to say. I mean we are speechless!" I said as we were trying to take it all in.

"Yes, Bruce, we will go through the motorhome and get it ready for you. You can pick it up in two days," Doug said.

We left the dealership stunned, still not believing what was happening. We came back to the dealership two days later, and they had it ready.

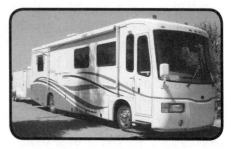

We still were in shock over the whole ordeal as we left the dealership and started home in this new motorhome. I still could not believe that we were driving this thing home!

"Diane, can you believe this? Is this really happening?" I said to my wife in shock!

"Bruce, I still can't believe this. God has answered our prayers, but in a way that was totally unexpectedly awesome! God, you are so good to us!" Said Diane.

We were about one hour into the two hour trip, and the Lord quickened my mind to the car we had given my sister Janine, a few years before. I could feel the Lord speaking to my heart, "Bruce, remember that car you gave your sister, do you really think you can out-give Me?" The Lord said as he impressed it on my heart.

"Diane! Remember that car we gave Janine! The Lord spoke to my heart and said that we can't out-give HIM!" I said with excitement.

"Bruce, I felt the same thing!"

At that moment, we both said a prayer, "Lord, You are so good to us. We haven't done anything to deserve this blessing. Thank you!"

We ended up driving that motorhome for close to five-years and put over 200,000 miles on it. After we were done with that motorhome, we used it as a trade in on our MCI bus that we currently drive.

Listen up, for I want you to get this. The Lord wants you to show love just like Him! He wants us to have a heart to be a miracle in the lives of others. When Diane and I decided that we wanted to be a miracle    to my sister, Janine, by giving her that car, little did we realize that we were setting ourselves up for the biggest miracle that we had ever experienced in terms of a material need for our ministry. That is God's marvelous plan of economy. We found out something about God that day. You can certainly try, but you can't out-give the Him. Our Father in Heaven has a bigger heart than we do, and He loves to be a blessing to His children. The hundredfold blessing is God's marvelous plan of economy!

APPLICATION:
CHAMPIONS SHOW LOVE BY GIVING

In Code #1, we showed you the Ten Commandments in pictures. We gave them to you in picture form so that you could memorize them. The pictures make it easy for you, but I have even better news! If you have a problem memorizing them even with the pictures, God in His wisdom did something in the New Testament to make it even easier. God took the Ten Commandments and defined them in terms of Love. Love is the key to obeying the commandments! It is really simple. God wants us to first show love to Him, and then show love to others.

> "Jesus answered him, 'And you shall love the LORD your God with all your heart, with all your soul, with all your mind, and with all your strength. This is the first commandment. And the second, like it, is this: You shall love your neighbor as yourself. There is no other commandment greater than these'" (Mark 12:29-31).

When you obey these two commandments you will obey all Ten Commandments. When you do, God will bless you!

God wants to bless His children, but God's economy is not about what God can do for us, it is also about what we can do for God! What can we do for God? JUST OBEY HIM! If you read Deuteronomy chapter 28, God says that when we obey him, there are 14 verses of blessings that God wants to give the person who obeys.

> "Now it shall come to pass, if you diligently obey the voice of the LORD your God, to observe carefully all His commandments which I command you today, then the LORD your God will set you high above all the nations of the earth. And all these blessings shall

come upon you and overtake you, because you obey the voice of the LORD your God. (Deut. 28)

If you will read all the way through verse 14 in that chapter, you will find that God will bless every area in the life of the obedient person. Every person loves to be a recipient of God's blessings. Many will spend all their time hunting for the blessings of God, but if we will look at Deuteronomy 28, we will not have to go looking for the blessings of God. When we give God our love and obedience, and love others as ourself, it says that **"all of these blessings will come upon you and overtake you."** In modern terms, that means that the blessings of God are going to find us and **RUN US OVER!**

Now does God bless His children so that they can have a lot of neat stuff? **NO, God has two reasons for blessing His children: 1) Because He loves His children. 2) So that His children can be a blessing to back to God, and to others!**

THE HUNDREDFOLD BLESSING

Many times when we give, we want to know, "What's in it for me?" If there is no return, then it can be difficult to give. Here are two eye opening verses:

> "'Bring all the tithes into the storehouse, that there may be food in My house, and try Me now in this,' says the Lord of hosts, 'If I will not open for you the windows of heaven and pour out for you such blessing that there will not be room enough to receive it'" (Malachi 3:10).

"Assuredly, I say to you, there is no one who has left house or brothers or sisters or father or mother or wife or children or lands, for My sake and the gospel's, who shall not receive a hundredfold now in this time—houses and brothers and sisters and

mothers and children and lands, with persecutions—and in the age to come, eternal life" (Mark 10:29-30).

When we blessed Janine with that car, we didn't realize the magnitude of God's economy! There are some who would say that our motivation for giving should be because it is the right thing to do. Yes, this is true it is the right thing to do but after reading these two verses, it sounds like giving to God and to others would be a good investment. Now we have heard of investing in the stock market so that we can get a return on our money. If we were to get a 10% - 20% return, that would be considered a really good investment by Wall Street standards. But there may be a better place to put our investment dollars!

We just read words like, "such a blessing that there will not be room enough to receive it," and getting "a hundredfold" blessing. It all sounds too good to be true.

In the verse in Malachi, it is talking about giving money, and in the Mark 10 verse, it is talking about giving up things, like family and lands for the sake of the Gospel. I've come to the conclusion, that no matter what we give, time, talent, things, or finances, when it has to do with the Kingdom of God, there will be a return, and not just any return, but an "out of this world" return! But I want you to notice the phrase in the verse, "with persecutions". That little phrase says that yes, you will get a great return on your money, but there will be a cost. Jesus said that you will suffer persecutions for following Him and investing into His Kingdom. Jesus never said it would be easy, but once again, it is worth it all!

HUNDREDFOLD?

With this hundredfold return, there are two ways to look at it. When you hear of the word Hundredfold, we think some number times 100. God's wealth is infinite.

If you give according to what you have, you will always come short. But if you give according to what God has, this concept will revolutionize your life.

This hundredfold blessing will either be times one hundred, or exponentially, times one hundred. Let me explain. If you gave $1.00 to help your church, or help someone in need, and you take that times 100, you will get a return of $100. But if you noticed, Jesus used the term "a hundredfold" to explain God's wealth. If you take a sheet of paper, you basically have one layer of paper, but if you fold it over once, you have two layers. If you fold it again, you have four layers. If you fold if again, you have eight layers; again, you have sixteen. Do you see what is happening? Every time you fold it, you double your return.

I have a question for you. Would you rather have $1,000,000, or would you rather receive one penny, and I let you double that every day for a month? If you take the million, you are losing out. If you said a penny and double it every day for a month, that is the correct answer! If you take a penny and double it every day for 31 days, you will have $21,474,836.48! Listen to this, after 50 days, you will have over eleven, yes, eleven trillion dollars, 11,258,999,068,462 to be exact. If you try to keep going to get to one hundred, you will have a tough time figuring out the amount, for most calculators will not calculate the number, because the number is so large!

Diane and I certainly haven't given like we should, but what little we have given, we have seen God's miraculous provision in our lives. The point is this, God owns everything! He owns all the wealth of the world. He wants His children to learn of His plan of economy! He wants us to invest in His Kingdom. The secret to getting rich is not rocket science, it is one word. GIVE! When we give, we have His promise that we will receive a return because He loves His Children!

PICTURES FROM AROUND THE WORLD

LONDON, CHINA, NEW YORK, YOSEMITE, AFRICA, HUNGARY, MILWAUKEE, ELKTON

Code #7

CODE #7
CHAMPIONS TAKE CARE OF THE GIFTS THE LORD HAS GIVEN THEM.

"Every good gift and every perfect gift is from above, and comes down from the Father of lights, with whom there is no variation or shadow of turning" (James 1:17).

"Then Peter said to them, 'Repent, and let every one of you be baptized in the name of Jesus Christ for the remission of sins; and you shall receive the gift of the Holy Spirit'" (Acts 2:38).

"A man's gift makes room for him, And brings him before great men" (Proverbs 18:16).

"If you then, being evil, know how to give good gifts to your children, how much more will your heavenly Father give the Holy Spirit to those who ask Him!" (Luke 11:13)

"But to each one of us grace was given according to the measure of Christ's gift. Therefore He says: 'When He ascended on high, He led captivity captive, And gave gifts to men.' And He Himself gave some to be apostles, some prophets, some evangelists, and some pastors and teachers, for the equipping of the saints for the work of ministry, for the edifying of the body of Christ" (Ephesians 4:7-12).

"As iron sharpens iron, so a man sharpens the countenance of his friend" (Proverbs 27:17).

THE POWER OF INFLUENCE

God has blessed everyone with gifts. James shares with us that every good and perfect gift comes down from God. Our bodies, our minds, our spirits, our talents and abilities, these all come from God. It is up to us to take care of them and develop them, and to encourage others to do the same. My awareness of this responsibility started when I was just a kid.

STORY
ONE MORE PUSH-UP

"Hey Tanya, there are a couple guys at Ashland College, Jay Hoover and 'Crazy' George Schauer, both of these guys can spin a basketball on their finger. But listen to this, Crazy George does a basketball spinning show. He can also do some cool tricks with the basketball! As a matter of fact, Crazy George can spin two basketballs at the same time!" Maurice our oldest brother said to his younger sister, Tanya, while he was on break from college.

"Wow, I love basketball, and that would be something fun to practice. The more things that I can learn with the basketball, the better I will become." Tanya said as she grabbed a basketball.

Tanya practiced and not only learned how to spin it, but eventually got really good at it. She later met George Schauer at a basketball camp. When she did, George taught her some other basketball handling and dribbling skills. This had a large impact not only on Tanya, but also indirectly me. I have never met Crazy George, but his influence changed the course of our family.

When I was just 7-years-old, I was intrigued by the spinning and other things that Tanya had learned with the basketball. This curiosity led to a desire to learn, and I literally became my sister Tanya's shadow. I would see her practicing in the garage, so I would try to practice. I was so little at the time, I mostly got in the way, but I was eager to learn, and she was patient enough with me to teach me.

"Tanya, can you teach me how to spin a basketball?" I said with expectation.

"Yes, Bruce. Grab the basketball like this with two hands, flip it in the air like this to get the ball spinning, and put your index finger on the bottom of the ball. Try to practice this over and over." She said as she handed me the ball.

"Thanks Tanya, I will give it a try!" I said with that little kid determination.

After watching her do it so effortlessly, it had to be easy, right? Wrong I flipped the basketball just like she did, and it missed my finger by a long shot. I did it again, and it missed again. I did it one more time, and it landed on my finger, but it really hurt. I came to the conclusion that spinning a basketball on your finger may look cool, but learning can be a painful endeavor!

As the story goes, I used to practice so much that I got a blister on the end of my finger from spinning it

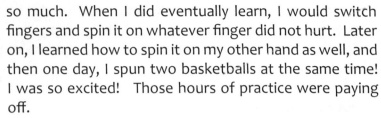

so much. When I did eventually learn, I would switch fingers and spin it on whatever finger did not hurt. Later on, I learned how to spin it on my other hand as well, and then one day, I spun two basketballs at the same time! I was so excited! Those hours of practice were paying off.

During the time I was practicing with the basketball, my brother Ray came home from college. Ray was on the floor doing push-ups. I was counting them in my mind, "forty-six, forty-seven, forty-eight, forty-nine, fifty, fifty-one?" "What? Uhhh, good job, Ray!" I said to my brother, with a questioning look.

While Ray was home from the United States Naval Academy, he was staying in my bedroom with me. He is 11-years older than me. My other brother Bert lived across the hall from me in our house in one of the back bedrooms. Every night before bed, both Ray and Bert would do a little workout in my room.

Ray and Bert were fun brothers, and they really had my respect. For their workout, Ray was doing some push-ups and sit-ups, just to stay in shape. While Ray was doing his push-ups, he aroused my curiosity.

"Excuse me Ray, I have a question for you." I inquired. "When you were doing your push-ups, I was counting them in my mind as you did them, and I counted 51 push-ups. Did I miscount, or were you trying to do that many?"

"Yes, Bruce, you are right, you didn't miscount. I meant to do that many," Ray said as he knelt down to do another set of push-ups.

"But Ray, most people, when they do some push-ups, they usually do an even number, like 50 push-ups. Why did you do 51?"

"You see, little brother, it was my goal to do 50, but I did one more for extra effort. That's why you counted 51. I always try to push myself, even when I am all alone."

"But how can one push-up make you that much stronger?"

"Doing one push-up is not that big of a deal, but it is where you place that one push-up, that's what makes it a big deal. The extra push-up is never at the beginning of the set, it is always placed at the very end of the set. This is when you are most tired and you feel like quitting. When I get to my goal of 50 push-ups, I push myself to do an extra one when it is the toughest, and I don't feel like it. This does something to my attitude. It gives me a tenacity and I really like it!" He explained as a new idea formed in my little mind.

"Well, Ray, I really like the idea too. I think I am going to add the extra effort to my life as well," I added.

After Ray finished his push-ups, I pulled out a small piece of yellow paper. On the paper I wrote, 20 push-ups and I tacked it up on a little bulletin board in my room. That night, before I jumped into bed, I did some push-ups, too. Do you know how many push-ups I did? You got it right, I did twenty-one!

When I was in the 7th grade, the Rickers, came to our house over the 4th of July. They were our first cousins who lived about a seven-hour drive from our house. Lance Ricker was three years older than me, and was a great athlete. When he came over, we would hang out together.

When they came to visit, Lance brought something with him that would later change the course of my life. That something was, a unicycle. I had never seen a unicycle in person, and only had seen someone ride one at a circus. Lance had learned to ride the unicycle, and he rode that one wheeled contraption all over our yard like it was nothing! After seeing how easy he made it look, I was so fascinated by that thing, that I just had to try it. I had the attitude that if my cousin could do it, then I should be able to do it!

"Lance, can I try to ride that unicycle?" I said with

anticipation.

"Sure, Bruce, you can try, but you won't be able to do it right away," Lance said as he was speaking from experience.

"Oh, if you can do it, it can't be that hard," I said as I confidently grabbed it by the seat.

So, being a determined 13-year-old, I got on the seat, placed my feet on the pedals, grabbed Lance by the shoulder, pushed off and tried to pedal and, WHAM! I immediately fell on my back!

"Ha ha ha ha! Bruce, I told you! It is not as easy as it looks! You are going to have to spend a lot more time than that practicing. It took me about a week of practicing every day to get it right." Lance said as he laughed.

Being determined to not give up so easily, I got back on, tried it again, and I fell again, and again, and again. I kept falling and spent most of that day either on my back or with my butt on the ground. With scratches, bruises, and being very frustrated, I came to the conclusion that riding the unicycle was nothing like riding a bike, and was actually a lot harder than it looked.

It was the Monday after the 4th of July, and the Rickers were packing up and leaving that afternoon. As their family was getting ready, I was getting in just a little more practice on Lance's unicycle before they left.

"Hey, Lance, thanks so much for bringing your unicycle and for letting me try to learn. I didn't get it and have a long way to go, but maybe next time you come, you can bring it with you, and I will try it again!" I said as they loaded up.

"Bruce, here you go," Lance said as he lifted up his unicycle toward me. "I want you to have this unicycle!"

"What? Are you kidding? Really, Lance? Are you giving me your unicycle?" I said not believing what I was hearing.

"Yes, Bruce, I really want you to learn. I have

another unicycle at home. I really like riding it, and when you learn, you will like riding it as well!" Lance said as he handed it to me.

After Lance gave me that unicycle, I literally spent the next four days practicing morning to evening and was either on that unicycle seat or on the ground. After the third day, I was seeing less of the ground and more of the seat. The many falls, bruises and scrapes, were trophies to the value of determination, for I learned how to ride that one wheeled contraption, and it was a testimony to the generosity of a cousin.

I wasn't expecting to receive that gift, but God was putting the pieces of the puzzle together. He knew that down the road, over 30 years later, Lance's influence and generosity would be a huge puzzle piece in my family's quest in making it to the finals of *America's Got Talent*.

APPLICATION:

Take care of the gifts that God has given you! The greatest gift that God gives believers is the gift of the Holy Spirit. We need the Holy Spirit in our lives to do The Champion Codes! Without God's power in our lives, living for Him is impossible! As the Spirit gave the New Testament believers power to be Champions for God, He will do the same thing for you!

It says in Scripture, **"And whatever you do, do it heartily, as to the Lord and not to men,"** (Col. 3:23) Don't give God the scraps off your table. Give Him your best! Jesus gave everything for you, and He is worthy of your full effort. Because of what God has done for you, He is the only one worthy of receiving extra effort. If you make it a point to give extra effort for God, He will bless you and make everything you do prosper! It will have a stamp of excellence.

Never underestimate the power of influence! I didn't realize it, but doing extra effort on a silly push-up

started carrying over into other areas of my life as well. When I started giving extra effort when nobody was watching, giving extra effort when other people were watching was easy because it was becoming a habit. This extra effort not only helped me, but it also carried over into our family. Now, Diane and I see our kids giving extra effort!

God has blessed you with the gift of your spirit, your body and your talents! Develop them! If you had told me when I was younger, Bruce, some day you are going to be traveling all over the world performing with basketballs, in front of millions of people, not just by yourself, but with your wife, Diane, and your twelve children, as a witness for God, I would have thought you were crazy. Traveling around the world was not my goal. I figured that if God blessed me with gifts, then I was going to practice and develop those gifts to the best of my ability.

Today, there are so many kids and adults who are so caught up watching TV or playing video games, that they never develop their God given talents. God has blessed every person with something, and every person has something to offer. Don't be a spectator in life and sit around watching everyone live their lives. Get into the game and develop your talents, start giving extra effort, so that when you are called to play in life's game, you have something to offer!

When you get into life's game and make extra effort a way of life, your life will take on a whole new meaning! Your life will be a life of Excellence! What is Excellence? **EXCELLENCE IS THE EXCEPTIONAL QUALITY TO EXCEED EXPECTATIONS.**

CHAMPIONS CHOOSE THE DIFFICULT PATH

"Enter by the narrow gate; for wide is the gate and broad is the way that leads to destruction, and there are many who go in by it. But narrow is the gate and difficult is the way which leads to life, and there are few who find it." (Matt. 7:13-14)

CHOOSING THE DIFFICULT PATH

Jesus said there are two paths that people travel in life. The wide way, and the narrow way; the easy way, and the hard way. Many things in this life are geared to make life more convenient, easier and more comfortable. But when it comes to following God, He wants us out of our comfort zone. This reminds me of the of the story in Matthew 14:25-33 when Jesus walked on the water:

"Now in the fourth watch of the night Jesus went to them, walking on the sea. And when the disciples saw Him walking on the sea, they were troubled, saying, 'It is a ghost!' And they cried out for fear. But immediately Jesus spoke to them, saying, 'Be of good cheer! It is I; do not be afraid.' And Peter answered Him and said, 'Lord, if it is You, command me to come to You on the water.' So He said, 'Come.' And when Peter had come down out of the boat, he walked on the water to go to Jesus. But when he saw that the wind was boisterous, he was afraid; and beginning to sink he cried out, saying, 'Lord, save me!' And immediately Jesus stretched out His hand and caught him, and said to him, 'O you of little faith, why did you doubt?' And when they got into the boat, the wind ceased. Then those who were in the boat came and worshiped Him, saying, 'Truly You are the Son of God.'" (Matt. 24:25-33)

WHATEVER YOU DO, DON'T GET WET!

As I read this story one day, the Lord gave me a revelation about stepping out of our comfort zone. If you have never made a commitment to Christ, it is like you are standing on the dock of the world. It seems safe, because you are next to land, but it is not. God calls you to get into the Christian boat, for you need to get to the other side! When you make a commitment to Christ, you have stepped off the dock of the world, and are now in the Christian boat. You are headed to the other side which figuratively is heaven.

After getting into the boat, you get strapped into your seat, and you become comfortable as a Christian. As you ride in the Christian boat, storms may come up, waves will hit you, but that's OK, because you counted the cost. You knew that things would be harder, but you have God's promise that you will make it to the other side.

All of the sudden, you are startled to see Jesus out on the water walking toward the boat! You are frightened by His appearance for something like that has never happened before. As He gets close, He starts walking past and He looks right at you. He motions with His hand for you to join Him on the water. You see his invitation and you respond with, "What? Who me? You want me out there on the water?"

So you tell a couple other Christian friends sitting next to you, that Jesus was motioning with His hand for you to come out on the water. You share with them that you are going to go for it, and join Him. All your friends just laugh at you and make fun of you for thinking such a silly thought. They say: "You better not do it. He's the Son of God and that is expected of Him. No regular human has ever done it before. If you try, you are going to get WET and will probably drown. If you don't drown, you will most likely get hurt and look like an idiot for trying!"

So you end up agreeing with them that it was a silly idea. You sit back and get strapped into your comfortable Christian boat, because you certainly don't want to get WET!

Sadly, because of this fear of getting WET, you will end up living a life of mediocrity.

But this doesn't have to be the story of your life! In the story about Jesus walking on the water, what people don't realize is this: Before he started sinking, Peter WALKED on the WATER! He did something that no other person on earth had done besides Jesus! He had victory because he was willing to step out of His comfort zone and get WET for His King.

Every now and then we are given an opportunity to step out on the water where Jesus is walking. People may make fun of you and discourage you. These may be people who claim to know Christ! Walking on the water with Jesus will change your comfortable Christian experience into a more difficult path. When you do, you will most likely get WET, but you may find yourself doing something no one else has done before. Walking on water may seem impossible, but I have news for you! Matthew 19:26 says: **"With God, all things are possible."**

THE CHAMPION CODE

Code #1: Champions make sure their name is in the book of life. What does it profit a man if he gains the whole world and yet loses his soul in hell? If your name is not in God's book by the time you die, then you have lived your life in foolishness. It probably would have been better had you not been born. If you prayed to make Jesus Lord of your life, you are now a member of God's family! You are a new creature! So live like it!

Code #2: Champions get to know Jesus Christ. After you get your name into God's Book of Life, you are going to want to learn about and get to know this God who created you and loved you so much that He died in

your place. Spend time and listen to God's voice. Oh, you can't hear his voice? If you can't hear God's voice, it is because you've got too many voices in your life! Shut off the TV, the computer, the ipod, the facebook, and the phone. God is talking to you, are you listening? He won't be shouting, according to 1 Kings 19:12, God speaks in a still small voice.

Code #3: Champions make Jesus Christ known to the lost and dying world. As you get to know God the Father, Jesus the Son, and the Holy Spirit, you are going to get part of their heart and catch the vision. What is that vision? According to Luke 19:10, Jesus came to seek and save the lost. His burden will become your burden and you will want to start telling others the good news. Don't be afraid, because you have the five qualifications to share your faith, plus you have His powerful Word. Expect results because the quality is in the seed and not the sower!

Code #4: Champions build their lives on the Rock of God's Word. As you have the desire to share the good news, you will need a foundation. You will become a wise man, because you will have heard, read, studied, memorized, meditated, and applied God's Word to your life. When the storms of life come your way, you are going to be a powerhouse faith machine! When you want to share the good news with someone else, you will know exactly what to say, because you have built your life on the Rock of God's Word!

Code #5: Champions become overcomers by defeating temptations and trials. As you read God's word, you will be encouraged, and it will reveal areas in your life that need work. You are going to become an overcomer by the blood of the Lamb and the words of your testimony. In this section you are going to do what Jesus did to defeat the devil in your life, you are going to confess to God, to yourself, to the world, and to the devil, Scripture based confessions of who you are in the eyes of God. And who are you? A Champion!

Code #6: Champions show love by giving of their time, talent and finances to God and others. As you overcome, God's love will fill your heart, and you will have a desire to show that love back to God and to others by giving. God's wealth is infinite, and this same wealthy God just happens to be your Father who loves you sooooooo much! Don't give based on what's in your bank account, give based on what's in God's bank account! As you obey Him, He is going to find you, run you down and bless the socks off of you!

Code #7: Champions take care of the gifts that the Lord has given them. God will give you a desire to take care of the many gifts that God has given you. He's given you the gift of your body, your spirit, the Holy Spirit, your family, and your friends. If you want to make your life meaningful here on earth and also make it count for eternity, today is the day to start being the Champion that God intended you to be! You will not be able to do this on your own. Ask God to fill you with His Holy Spirit so that you will have the power to take care of all the gifts that God has given you. You can do it! God will give you strength! Take care of your body. God gave it to you, but most of you treat it like garbage. Stop eating junk food and start exercising! Parents spend time with your kids! Kids stop being disrespectful to your parents. If you want to be blessed, then you better honor them. Read the fifth commandment.

THE FIVE POUND PIECE OF STEEL

God has created you to be a Champion! The devil wants you to be a loser. God doesn't force anyone to be a part of His Championship Team, but the invitation is for everyone. If you want to be on His Team, you will have to count the cost.

In Matthew 25:14, we are given the parable of the talents. God has given each person certain abilities. He

wants us to do something with what He has given us.

This reminds me of an illustration that I heard: If I had a piece of steel that weighed 5 pounds, it would be worth about $5. If I do nothing, it will only be worth $5. But if I decide to put a little work into the steel by melting it down and putting it in a mold, I could form it into horseshoes now worth $20. Lets say, I melt it down and decide to make table knives. It is now worth about $100. Say I melt it down and make sewing needles. The 5 pounds of steel is now worth $5000. But if I get really creative, put extra time and effort into it, I can melt it down and make tiny springs for fine Swiss watches. This will take work, but that five-pound piece of steel that used to be worth $5 is now worth $200,000. This is all from that same piece of steel!

Each of us is like that piece of steel. Scripture says in Psalms 139:14, that we are fearfully and wonderfully made. There is so much potential in each person, but the devil doesn't want you to know how special you really are to God. Actually, the devil has three plans for your life. According to John 10:10, he comes to steal, kill, and destroy. He wants to steal God's plan for your life. He wants to destroy all your relationships, and if that is not bad enough, he wants to kill you. That doesn't sound like a fun plan. If you to sit back and be passive and not do anything, his plan will most likely start coming to pass in your life. He wants you to think and say negative things about God, yourself and others. If you keep thinking and saying worthless things, then you will end up being worthless. But it doesn't have to be that way.

ENTHUSIASM IS THE KEY

We meet kids and adults who are on the Championship road. But we also meet many others who are so depressed, that they want to end their life. Don't be so foolish! You may not feel special in the eyes of the world, but you are so special to God. If you want a breakthrough in your life, your circumstances may not immediately change, but you can change your thoughts, your attitude, and your words. Get some enthusiasm for life.

The word enthusiasm comes from the Greek word, "<u>Entheos</u>". <u>Entheos</u> comes from two words: <u>En</u> meaning within and <u>Theos</u> meaning Spirit. It literally means "God within". When you get God within your life, He will give you an excitement and passion for life and for whatever you set out to accomplish. Think of enthusiasm as excitement and power that is under control!

You may not feel enthusiastic, but you can't let your feelings run your life. Don't be ruled by your feelings, rather be ruled by the facts in God's Word! If you feel like you are on the losing team, that can change starting today by taking initiative. Choose to have enthusiasm and let God's powerful Word work in your life. When you practice The Champion Code with Enthusiasm, you will get results!

WHEN DO I START? WHAT DO I DO?

Today is the day to start a change of direction. One thing that I appreciate about God is that **God never consults your past to determine your future. I will say that again! GOD NEVER CONSULTS YOUR PAST TO DETERMINE YOUR FUTURE.**

Dwelling on the past can produce guilt and remorse. Dwelling on the future can produce fear and doubt. But when you concentrate on the present, you can decide right now to be a Champion. Don't worry about the past and don't worry about your future. You can change neither of them. The one thing you can change is your attitude right now! You can do it!

To start, you must change the way you think. We are commanded in Philippians 4:8 **"Finally, brethren, whatever things are true, whatever things are noble, whatever things are just, whatever things are pure,**

whatever things are lovely, whatever things are of good report, if there is any virtue and if there is anything praiseworthy—meditate on these things."

Champions think thoughts that are encouraging, positive, and uplifting. Don't believe what the devil or the world says about you. Start believing what God says about you. What does God think about you? Jeremiah 29:11 says: **"For I know the thoughts that I think toward you, says the LORD, thoughts of peace and not of evil, to give you a future and a hope."** God's thoughts toward you will give you a positive future and a hope! Isn't that exciting!

If you want your circumstances to change, you must change what you say. You must speak the word of faith and feed your nervous system a vocabulary of constructive, progressive, productive and victorious words. When you do, those powerful words will begin to change you and the things around you. When you regularly confess with your mouth what God says about you, faith springs up in your spirit. Why is this? Because faith comes by hearing, and hearing by the Word of God! (Romans 10:17) When we apply faith to a problem, good things will happen.

In Code Number 5, we found out that words are powerful. Your speech center in your brain affects all the nerves in your body. To be a Champion and to have a breakthrough in your life you must not only meditate and think like a Champion, but you need to start talking like a Champion. Scripture says: **"Fight the good fight of faith, lay hold on eternal life, to which you were also called and have confessed the good confession in the presence of many witnesses" (I Timothy 6:12).** The good confession God wants you to say is what He thinks and says about you! When you watch a basketball or football game, you see cheerleaders cheering on their team. Throughout the whole game they are speaking positive and uplifting words to encourage the players. Did you know that God is your cheerleader! He is speaking positive words to you and is cheering for you. He wants you to win. But like that $5 piece of steel, if you want to convert it to something else, you are going to have to work at it. The more work you put into it, the more value you will get out of it. If you want your circumstances to change, you have to work at it and start changing what you think and what you say!

Finally, **if you want to be a Champion and you want your circumstances to change, you must change what you do.** It says in James 1:25: **"But he who looks into the perfect law of liberty and continues in it, and is not a forgetful hearer but a doer of the work, this one will be blessed in what he does."** We serve the God of the breakthrough, and if you want to blessed, you must be a doer of the work. God will do His part, but He gives you a responsibility to do your part! If you walk around thinking and confessing negative ideas, these thoughts and words will start carrying over into your actions, and you will not get very far in life. To turn the tide, we have included some prayers and also some positive confessions from God's word.

THINK, TALK, AND ACT LIKE A CHAMPION

There are many Scriptures that pertain to every circumstance. To start you on your journey to having victory in your life, we have included the following confessions. Read the following Scripture based prayers and confessions and underline those parts that may pertain to your situation. Then meditate on them and confess them aloud several times per day.

Prayer: Father in Heaven, I come to you in the Name of Jesus. Father, thank you for sending your Son Jesus for dying in my place. Thank you that You were buried and You rose from the grave. Thank you, Jesus, for writing my name in the Book of Life. Jesus thank you for sending your Holy Spirit to empower my life to live for

You. Fill me with your Spirit so that I can do the seven things that Champions do before they die. Help me to make my life count for You. Lord I praise You for who You are and who You are making me to be. Help me to know You and worship You like I should. Help me to be a witness through my words and my actions to my family, my friends, and to other people that may come my way. Please give me a hunger for Your Word so that I can grow to become more like You. Help me to overcome the temptations and trials that weigh me down. Please give me an opportunity to show my love by giving my time, talent and finances to God and to others, knowing that You will provide for me. Thank you for the gifts You have given me. Thank you for my body, my spirit, the Holy Spirit, my family and my friends. Help me to take care of them. In Jesus name, Amen!

CONFESSIONS OF CHAMPIONS

Pray to God, and start talking like the Champion that God has made you to be. Say the following Scripture based confessions and prayers daily:

As Jesus used the word of God to have victory over the devil in the wilderness, I too will use the word of God to have victory in my life. What God says in His word about me, I believe! I accept His appraisal as the final truth, and I refuse any report, symptom or feeling to the contrary.

God's word is powerful, active and sharp. It will bring about positive changes in me.

My body is the temple of the Holy Spirit who is in me, whom I have from God. I will be led by God because I am not my own? (I Cor.6:19)

I have this confidence in Him, that if I ask anything according to His will, He hears me. If I know that He hears me, I know that I have that which I asked of him. (1 John 5:14-15)

I have peace with God through Jesus Christ. (Rm. 5:10)

I am crucified with Christ, and I no longer live, but Christ lives in me, the life I now live in the body, I live by faith in the Son of God, who loves me and gave His life for me. (Gal. 2:20)

Sin is no longer my master. (Romans 6:14)

My mind is being transformed by God's word, therefore, I offer my body as a living sacrifice, so that I can be holy and acceptable to God. I am not conformed to this world, but I am being transformed by the renewing of my mind. Now I can test and approve what God's perfect will is for my life. (Rm. 12:1-2)

I am a new creature because of what God has done for me. (2 Cor. 5:17)

I have overcome the devil by the blood of the Lamb and by the word of my testimony. (Rev. 12:11)

I belong to God. (John 17:9)

God has given me exceedingly great and precious promises through which I am a partaker of the divine nature, having escaped the corruption that is in the world. (2 Peter 5:4)

I am protected by the power of God's Name. (John 17:11)

I have been born of God, and have overcome the world. This is the victory that has overcome the world, even my faith. (1 John 5:4)

I have been set free from the law of sin and death. (Rm. 8:2)

If God is for me, who can be against me? He has freely given me all things in Christ. (Rm 8:31-32)

I have been bought with a price, therefore I glorify God in my body. (1 Cor. 6:20)

I have the mind of Christ. (1 Cor. 2:16)

I am part of the chosen generation, the royal priesthood, His own special people, and I will proclaim the praises of Him who called me out of darkness into His marvelous light. (1 Peter 2:9)

He who began a good work in me will complete it!

(Phil 1:6)

I can do all things through Christ who gives me strength. (Phil. 4:13)

I am strong in the Lord, and the power of his might. (Eph. 6:10)

The Lord will deliver me from every evil work and preserve me for His Kingdom. (2 Tim. 4:18)

I am counting it all joy when I fall into various trials because I know that the testing of my faith produces perseverance. This will work toward my completeness and maturity. (James 1:2-4)

Jesus is able to keep me from stumbling and will present me faultless before the presence of His Glory with exceedingly great joy. To God my Savior, who alone is wise, be glory and majesty, dominion and power, both now and forever. Amen. (Jude 24-25)

Father in the Name of Jesus, I confess what You say concerning my healing. Just as Jesus healed every disease when He walked this earth, He also heals today. Therefore I believe in accordance with Your word that by Your Stripes, I am healed. Jesus took my infirmities and bore my sickness. Therefore based on God's word, I am redeemed from the curse of this sickness.

In Ephesians chapter six, Paul talks about putting on the whole armor of God.

> "For we do not wrestle against flesh and blood, but against principalities, against powers, against the rulers of the darkness of this age, against spiritual hosts of wickedness in the heavenly places. Therefore take up the whole armor of God, that you may be able to withstand in the evil day, and having done all to stand. Stand therefore, having girded your waist with truth, having put on the breastplate of righteousness and having shod your feet with the preparation of the gospel of peace; above all, taking the shield of faith with which you will be able to quench all the fiery darts of the wicked one. And take the helmet of Salvation, and the sword of the Spirit, which is

the word of God; praying always with all prayer and supplication in the Spirit, being watchful to this end with all perseverance and supplication for all the saints" (Eph. 6:12-18).

As Diane and I read through Scriptures, we found other important pieces of armor. One of the most important ones is the Cloak of Humility. As Christians, it is easy to shine our armor to the point where you can be so bright that those who are lost be blinded by our Christianity. Paul encourages us to become all things to all men that you might win some. That is why we need to put on the Ephesians six armor, and then over the top of that armor, put on the cloak of humility.

When we pray as a family we end our prayer by putting on the whole armor of God, starting with Ephesians 6:12-18:

PUTTING ON THE FULL ARMOR OF GOD
The Helmet of Salvation
Breastplate of Righteousness
The Belt of Truth
The feet fitted with the Gospel of Peace
The shield of Faith
And the Sword of the Spirit, which is the Word of God
At all times pray with Prayers and Petitions
Put on the cloak of humility

221

The Garment of Praise
May the Glory be our rear guard
Clothe us in the Lord Jesus Christ
Cloak of Zeal
Garment of Worship
The Mantle of Peace
Clothe us with Gladness
Clothe us with Light
Put on the new man
Put on the Gifts of the Spirit
And the Fruit of the Spirit,
Which are Love, Joy, Peace, Patience, Kindness, Goodness, Gentleness, Faithfulness and Self Control,
Put on the Hedge of Protection
The Mind of Christ
Rivers of Living Waters flowing our of our hearts
Righteousness, Justice and Liberty as a cloak
Crown us with loving kindness and tender mercies
Set a guard over the door of our lips
Blessings on our head
May we be worthy to escape the wrath to come
Pray singleness of heart
Fill us with your Spirit
Give us abundant Grace
Help us be the Salt of the Earth
The Bride of Christ
And pray for Wisdom and Courage
In Jesus Name, Amen!

Jacob Crevier does custom jewelry and repairs.
Contact him through:
Crevier Jewelry
crevierjewelry.com

TAKE YOUR PROGRAM TO NEXT LEVEL!

Bruce and Diane Crevier perform at schools, churches, basketball halftime shows, civic organizations, and corporate events. Bruce comes by himself, with some of the family, or all of the family. They can perform in large and small areas. To contact them or to order more books go to their website at: **championsforever.com** or through their address:

Champions Forever Ministries
21703 485th Ave.
Elkton, SD 57026 USA